Arthur Crump, Henry W. Rosenbaum

The Theory of Stock Exchange Speculation

Arthur Crump, Henry W. Rosenbaum

The Theory of Stock Exchange Speculation

ISBN/EAN: 9783337109424

Printed in Europe, USA, Canada, Australia, Japan

Cover: Foto ©ninafisch / pixelio.de

More available books at **www.hansebooks.com**

THE THEORY

OF

STOCK EXCHANGE

SPECULATION.

BY

ARTHUR CRUMP.

With Preface and Annotations by

H. W. ROSENBAUM.

NEW YORK:
H. W. ROSENBAUM.
1887.

PREFACE.

SOME years ago I came across a book, called "Crump's Theory of Stock Speculation," which had gone through several editions in England; and the practical wisdom expressed therein impressed me so forcibly that ever since then I formed the project of publishing an American edition.

The reader may be astonished that, as a broker, I desire to give such a book a larger circulation than it possessed heretofore, as the natural conclusion would be that it might injure my business. I feel, however, that it is not so, and think that a broker loses nothing by doing his duty in warning his clients against danger, and showing them the pitfalls.

I do not quite agree with the author of the book on every point, especially when he seeks to convey the impression that it would seem almost impossible that any profit could be derived from Stock Exchange speculation. During my long experience I have seen many speculators accumulate large fortunes, and I believe that when speculation is conducted by a clear-headed man, as a matter of business and not as a matter of amusement, it offers great chances.

Where the strength of Mr. Crump's work lies is in his showing what attributes of character a man must possess to be successful, and with these attributes a man must prove successful in stock speculation as well as in any other business. Condensed, these attributes are: first, a clear head; second, capital; and third, patience.

I do not agree with Mr. Crump, that a speculator, to be successful, must be a hard-hearted, selfish man. I found it different with most of the prominent men in Wall Street. Of course, if a Gould or a Vanderbilt buys up a whole railroad, he cannot very well take many people into his confidence; but these men are not what is generally called speculators—they are generals or diplomats, and they are not different in their actions from generals in warfare or diplomats in politics.

Outside of this class, I found generally, when I asked one of the prominent speculators for his opinion of the market, that he gave me his true and candid opinion of the future of the market; and the probabilities are that, if even not acting on this opinion at that very moment, his general policy was based on such a forecast of the market's condition.

The strength of the successful speculator lies in his observing the important principle set forth by Mr. Crump on page 60 of his work. "Speculators never set sufficient value on the importance of avoiding a loss—they think only of the profits." As it is with our money affairs when we say, "*Look after the pence; the pounds will take care of themselves*," so it is with speculation. Look after the losses; the profits will take care of themselves. Never refuse a profit, is a golden motto for speculators, which unhappily few of them, in their greediness, have the courage to adopt.' The observance of this rule is the main cause of the success of the best speculators, and the non-observance is the cause of failure of even their confidential friends.

Very few fortunes have been made in Wall Street at one stroke. Fortunes which were made in that way were generally lost again in a very short time. Most of the long, lasting, and solid fortunes were made by a gradual accumulation of profits extending over a great many years. The beginnings of these were sometimes quite small, and, as the capital increased, larger operations were entered into.*

Another cause of failure is the habit of taking larger risks than the means of speculators warrant. They naturally become nervous when they begin to see their capital dwindle away, and then begin, what is called in Wall Street, to "chip out." Now this is the curse of the speculator, not so much on account of the loss, as on account of the demoralization it will lead him into. Of course, big losses ought to be avoided, but at the same time well based and matured operations may sometimes be temporarily upset by a temporary manipulation of the market, or by some accidents which however right themselves in a few days, and cannot seriously interrupt the natural course of the market. In such a market a nervous speculator may "chip out" a fortune, and still be right in his views as to general conditions.

I think it is better to make one loss of 5 per cent. or so, when you know you are wrong, than to make three or five losses of 1 per cent. each, when you do

---

* In speaking of taking profits, the question arises, what is a profit ? Some people might say a profit is ½ per cent., and others 10 per cent. Now, of course, it is impossible to give an exact answer to this question. As a general rule, a transaction should not be made unless the chances of a gain are greater than the chances of a loss, but there may occasions occur when it would be advisable to take a small profit. All depends on the condition and temper of the market; but one rule I found to work well, and would recommend to every speculator, namely, that at the moment when a doubt arises in your mind, and you begin to ask yourself whether you ought to take your profit or not, then do not lose one moment's time, but take your profit, because you can never make a very serious mistake by doing so, while you might possibly make a very serious one by refusing it.

not know whether you are wrong or right, and in this connection Mr. Crump has very much undervalued the importance of options.

Options, if considered in their proper light, are the most important adjunct to speculation. They will enable the speculator to bridge over many difficulties, and furnish capital to speculators who know how to use them.

I do not say this simply because I am a broker in options, but because it is my honest conviction that options are cheap at almost any price, when a speculator has occasion to use them. If money is lost by buyers of options, it is because many of them are bought by people who have not sufficient reasons for doing so, and after the option has been bought, the owner does not know what to do with it. I have, for example, known people to be bulls on Lake Shore, and then go and spend money for a put in Western Union. Is it any wonder that men who do business on such principles lose money?

That many stock brokers object to options is natural. They look out for commissions, and greatly prefer to buy and sell several times a day on stop orders or on margins, even if customers lose money thereby, rather than see them make money two or three times a year, through operations extended over periods of two or three months each.

I do not mean to say that all stock brokers are of this kind, but if speculators recall their own experience, they will undoubtedly remember how often their broker said to them, "Cut your losses," if the transaction was against them, while, if the transaction showed a profit, the advice was, "Taking profits will never make any man poorer." All these things make commissions for the broker, and this is the object of his business.

Another reason for the unwillingness of some brokerage houses to encourage speculation against options must be found in the fact that a great many of them have not sufficiently large capital to enter upon large transactions without any other margin than the option. Although I acknowledge that it is hardly fair to ask a broker to do an unlimited amount of business based on options alone, the fact, nevertheless, exists that the strongest houses have always been glad to encourage trading against options, and only the more insignificant houses are opposed to it.

A well planned and matured operation, looking far ahead, backed by ample capital and patience, is the only way to make a fortune at the Stock Exchange, and prudence demands that in case the speculator's idea should have been wrong, he should have a safe way for a retreat open. Options will fulfill all these demands; and no matter how expensive, if the speculator can afford it, it is the only way of speculating in a safe and reasonable manner.

There are some people who are under the impression that they know everything already, and have nothing to learn, and such may be amused, but not benefited, by reading this book; others, however, who are inclined to speculate (and there are and always will be many of them) cannot fail to derive great benefit from the perusal of Mr. Crump's interesting work, and I hope I may put money in some people's pockets or save others from ruin by sending this book forth among the American people.

H. W. ROSENBAUM.

NEW YORK, Nov., 1886.

The last chapter in Mr. Crump's book, entitled "Outside Criticism on the Causes of Disturbance in the Money Market," has been omitted in this edition, as it relates simply to questions about the policy of the Bank of England in regard to regulating the discount rate, and a controversy and correspondence on this point between Mr. Crump and Mr. Bonamy Price.

As this whole question is of no practical value or interest to the American reader, I thought it expedient to omit the whole matter.

H. W. R.

CONTENTS.

CHAPTER I.

Technical Terms Explained.

		PAGE
1. Jobbers and Brokers	.	19
2. The Bull	.	19
3. The Bear .	.	19
4. Contango .	.	20
5. Backwardation	.	24
6. Options	.	26
7. The "Put and Call" Option	.	26
8. The "Put" Option	.	26
9. The "Call" Option .	.	26
10. The Fortnightly Settlement .	.	27
11. Speculation by Members of the House	.	28

CHAPTER II.

The Importance of Special Knowledge regarding the Regularly Recurring Causes that influence the Markets.

1. The Temper of the Public . . 32
2. Meteorological Influences . . 32
3. A Favorable Period of the Year . . 35
4. Causes affecting the Value of English Railway Stocks . 36
5. The Course to pursue at the Turn of the Half-year . . 36
6. Second Half of the Year more favorable for Bear Operations 37

Importance of Special Knowledge continued—

	PAGE
7. Activity among Buyers	39
8. The Bull Speculator's Great Chance	39
9. The great importance of being now and again altogether Clear of the Markets	40
10. The Movement of Prices near the Settlements	41

CHAPTER III.

The Right Temperament for a Professional Speculator.

1. Cool-headedness an indispensable Condition of Success . 43
2. The Uselessness of Haphazard Speculation . . . 45
3. Accurate Foresight 45
4. The Cool Man, or Professional Speculator . . . 46
5. Observance of the daily published Telegrams from abroad 46
6. The Selfishness and Hard-heartedness of the Professional Speculator 48
7. The Non-professional or Haphazard Speculator 50
8. The Misfortune of Early Gains . . . 55
9. Very few Failures made Public . 57
10. Greediness involves Loss . . 60
11. Keeping one's own Counsel . . 60

CHAPTER IV.

The Increase of Speculation in Stocks and Shares.

1. Stock Exchange Gambling increases in Europe, while Public Gaming-Houses are on the decline 62
2. Speculation an Out-growth of prosperous times . . 63
3. Commercial prosperity unhealthily fostered by Illegitimate Speculation 64
4. The Influence of Trade Profits upon the Stock Markets 64
5. An increase in the amount of Trade Profits realized, causes an Increase in the number of Securities . . . 65

The Increase of Speculations continued—

	PAGE
6. Speculation by Established Companies	66
7. The Demoralization caused by Temporary Success	66
8. The New Era in Speculation	67
9. Collapse through Over-speculation in Austria	67
10. Increase in the number of Members of the London Stock Exchange	68

CHAPTER V.

Modern Influences upon the Markets.

1. A Fixed Line of Action 71
2. Closer Uniformity of Values in all Markets through the Development of the Telegraph System . . . 72
3. A speculator cannot hope to succeed in any degree, unless his arrangements are as complete as those of a man engaged in *bona fide* business 73
4. The Diminution of Gluts in all Markets . . . 73
5. Modern conditions render it more difficult than formerly for Small Mercantile Houses to succeed . . . 73
6. Every Commercial Revulsion destroys Houses of a Speculative character, and throws the good business into the hands of the large sound Establishments . . . 75
7. The Extension of Long-wire Telegraphy 78
8. Money Famines should henceforth be as improbable of occurrence as Corn Famines 78
9. Advantages derived from opening up communications with the Corn-growing Provinces of Russia 80
10. The Growth of Wealthy Monetary Centres . . . 82
11. Private Cipher Telegrams as exterior influences upon Prices 83
12. The Altered Character of interior influences upon Prices 84
13. The Creation of Securities to meet the Demand . . 84
14. Getting behind the Scenes 85
15. The Difficulty of "Cutting" a Loss 85

CHAPTER VI.

Cacoëthes Operandi.

1. Waiting for Extremes	87
2. Reaction generally more rapid after a Sharp Rise	88
3. What Not To Do	90
4. Special Information	90
5. Much Money only obtainable as a certainty by Hard Work	90
6. An Average Instance of Haphazard Speculation	91

CHAPTER VII.

The Pit-falls.

1. Hidden Forces Opposed to the Speculator	94
2. The Turn	95
3. The Danger of taking Advice	95
4. A Disinterested Opinion	96
5. All the Eggs in One Basket	96
6. Traps for the Public	97
7. The Public as Speculators are Bulls by Nature	97
8. A Case of Roasting the Bulls	98
9. A Cut off the Loaf and Pass it on	98
10. Short Periods in, and Long ones out	99

CHAPTER VIII.

Speculation With Capital.

1. Restoring the Balance of Advantages	100
2. The Necessity of Some Capital	101
3. Capital to expend in Feints	102
4. La haute Finance	102
5. The Best of all Chances for a Speculator with Capital	103
6. The most Legitimate Form of Speculation, Pawning the Stock	104
7. When to Begin and when to Leave Off	105
8. Test of a Speculator's Pecuniary Position	105

CHAPTER IX.

Speculation Without Capital.

1. A Familiar Case		107
2. Bitter Experience		108
3. The Question of Seeing it Out		108

CHAPTER X.

The "Tip" to Buy or Sell.

1. A Friendly "Tip"		110
2. Unloading at other People's Expense		111
3. The Qualified "Tip"		111
4. The Unqualified "Tip"		112
5. "Tips" worked by Syndicates		112

CHAPTER XI.

Speculation by Machinery.

1. Machinery in existence for directing Human Volition		114
2. The Patrician Investor		115
3. Administering Shares to the Public		116

CHAPTER XII.

The Shifting of Speculation from the Higher to the Lower Classes of Securities.

1. Speculation in Consols as a Hedge		120
2. Speculation has Changed its Venue		121
3. Increase of the Indebtedness of the States of the World		121
4. The Fluctuations in the Price of Government Stocks		121
5. High Class Stocks more firmly held than formerly		122

CHAPTER XIII.

The Short "Turns," or who makes the Profits?

		PAGE
1.	The "Turn," a known quantity always against the Speculator	124
2.	The "Turn," a Loss in going into, and also in coming out of the Market	125
3.	The difference in the character of the "Turn," as compared with former times	125
4.	Special Danger of Speculating in a Stock that is quoted very wide	127
5.	The "Turn," the Income of the Jobber	128

CHAPTER XIV.

In what respect is Speculation useful in Markets generally?

1. Speculation for the Rise, which is both Legitimate and of Benefit to the Community . . . . . [129
2. Speculation for the Fall, which is both Legitimate and of Benefit to the Community 130
3. A Reasonable Relative Value for all Commodities . . 131
4. The Three Classes into which Speculators may be divided 132

INTRODUCTION.

Our object in writing this book is to endeavour to show to persons who may contemplate trying their hand at Stock Exchange speculation, the improbability of their hopes being realized. Much mischief and trouble would be avoided, and a deal of money saved, if, before entering upon such a dangerous career under the most favorable circumstances as that of a speculator, a study were made of the difficulties such an occupation involves, and also of the chances against the operator, considered as one individual *versus* the Stock markets. It is melancholy to think of the vast sums of money that are invested in the most serious sense of the word, annually by Stock Exchange speculators in the purchase of a sorrowful experience. It seems to be in the nature of things that numbers of people must come to grief in their early struggles, through an obstinate determination to trust complacently in their own ingenuity, in preference to profiting by the experience of others. A mountain climber who disclaims the aid of a guide, and is subsequently fished out of a crevasse, can expect no other epitaph, even from his friends, than that he has paid the deserved penalty of extreme temerity and folly. There are probably many guides who can ensure a safe passage over most mountain defiles, but he would be a bold man who guaranteed to pilot a young speculator through the Stock markets, and bring him out to a certainty with a profit.

If a speculator asks the advice of what we will term "an old hand," and it is in his interests to tell him what he really thinks, he will say: "Leave it alone."

Why so many people will never be convinced except by their own personal experience is, that they cannot believe what others say of things that are hidden.

"Hereof experience hath informed reason, and time hath made those things apparent which were hidden," says Sir W. Raleigh.

> " But apt the mind or fancy is to rove
> Uncheck'd, and of her roving is no end,
> Till warn'd, or by experience taught, she learns
> That not to know at large of things remote
> From use, obscure and subtle, but to know
> That which before us lies in daily life
> Is the prime of wisdom,"

says Milton; and

> " But if you'll prosper, mark what I advise,
> Whom age and long experience render wise,"

says Pope.

Stock Exchange speculation is very deceitful to the eye, and also to the ear. In some respects its associations are like those of a morass, under whose smooth and inviting surface are hidden the remains of unwary travellers. Those who are new to the business see only the glittering surface, and hear only of the fortunes made by stock brokers. People seldom tell of their losses.

Individuals who are tempted, not only by curiosity,

but by a love of excitement, and more than all in this case by the love of gain, go into the markets and lose their money, and quit the place with much the same feelings as the man who paid a penny to see a horse with his tail where his head ought to be.

"If we hope for things of which we have not thoroughly considered the value, our disappointment will be greater than our pleasure in the fruition of them," wrote Addison.

The most brilliant good fortune which may result from the operations of a speculator generally fall below his anticipations, when the operations are reduced to figures. It appears that the imagination gets, as it were, diseased by feeding on the contemplation of very rapid gains; and that whatever may be the reality of a hypothetical gain, the mind gets bewildered and fails to estimate as an element of loss, the surrounding husks in which the fruit is enclosed. One forgets that every tangible advantage, in whatever form obtained in this life, has to be got out of a shell. What, then, must be the speculator's feelings when the balance is on the wrong side of the account?

It has been suggested that the abolition of "time-bargains" would materially, if not quite, prevent much of the mischief that results from speculation; but it is no more possible entirely to do away with the custom of "time-bargains" than it is to abolish credit in other kinds of business. It may be readily conceded that a very large number of those who are ruined or greatly injured by Stock Exchange speculation, would never operate at all if they were called upon even to make a deposit before the purchase was effected. But when it is considered that to abolish "time-bargains" would be to ruin at once half the brokers in existence, the difficulty of effecting what from one point of view would be a most salutary change of custom, will be understood. In our day money is so closely employed that a fortnight is not too long to get the funds together, when, for some good reason or other, a change of investment has been determined on. It is often that such a transfer gives rise to a course of speculation that ends in disaster. A purchase effected for the account * with the view of changing from one stock to another leaves at the end of the fortnight, we will suppose, a handsome profit. The buyer of the stock takes it, and postpones the intended change of investment, thinking he shall get rich sooner by such an operation as that, than by simply transferring his money to another security that promised a better yield per cent. He has another try, expecting the same good fortune. In the end he loses as usual on balance, which he would not probably have done if he had bought and sold for money, finishing the operation on the same day. This is what often causes loss to people who can afford to lose, if they stop soon enough. The great mischief is done by the facilities afforded by "time-bargains" to operators who have a little money, just sufficient to enable them to keep afloat as speculators in fair weather. The first serious disturbance that violently agitates prices sweeps them away in a shoal.

The question which a sensible speculator will ask himself before he begins to operate is, What are the

---

* Where it says "for the account," it applies to the custom of the London Stock Exchange, where all the buying and selling is for the account, say generally the middle or end of the month.   H. W. R.

risks incurred of losing his all at one stroke? De Morgan, in his book on probabilities, says in Chapter V., on the risks of loss or gain, "A man should not hazard his all on any terms; but in ventures the loss of one of which would not be felt, we may suppose the venturer able to make a large number of the same kind; in which case the common notions of mankind reinforced by the results of theory, tell us that the sum risked must be only such a proportion of the possible gain as the mathematical probability of gaining it is of unity. For instance: suppose I am to receive a shilling if a die, yet to be thrown, give an ace; in the long run, an ace will occur one time out of six, or I shall lose five times for every time which I gain. I must, therefore, make one gain compensate the outlay of six ventures, or one-sixth of a shilling is what I may give for the prospect, one time with another. But one-sixth is the probability of throwing the ace. *Principle*—Multiply the sum to be gained by the fraction which expresses the chance of gaining it, and the result is the greatest sum which should be given for the chance."* "A man should not hazard his all on any terms." Does a man who enters upon a career of speculation take the trouble to consider at starting whether or not his first operation places him in a position in which he hazards his all? There is not probably one speculator in a hundred who ever thinks of it at all. We will suppose a man to be worth £200 in cash as his all, applicable to the payment of losses. It may safely be stated that num-

---

*According to this principle, operations conducted on options are more certain to result in profits in the long run than margin operations. If I assume to make a profit in only one out of every three operations, and each option costs me 1¼ per cent., I will make a profit, if the third option only yields me a profit of more than 3¾ per cent., which is nothing unusual. H. W. R.

bers of speculators open accounts with a less sum, in fact a considerable proportion of speculative operations are entered upon in reality without any funds at all; misfortunes in other vocations being frequently followed by gambling in the Stock markets. A speculator with £200 to pay losses with is in this position if he buys, for instance, for the rise £5,000 of any English railway stock; a fall of 5 per cent., which even in two or three days is nothing very extraordinary, carries him £50 "under water." What can he reckon upon on the other side, by keeping the account open, that is a mathematical certainty like the occurrence of an ace one time out of six in the long run in throwing the die? If he be exposed to such a loss at any moment as that mentioned, the risk is an absurd one to run if there is not at least an equal chance of a similar rise, and several times £250 in reserve. But all experienced in Stock Exchange fluctuations know that upward movements are, as a rule, gradual, a rise of 1 per cent. being considered as a profit which a speculator should without hesitation take, while a fall all round in a market of two or three per cent. in a day is of more common occurrence.* It may here, perhaps, be retorted that if a fall of 5 per cent. is nothing very extraordinary to happen in a few days, while a rise is, as a rule, gradual, why not speculate for the fall? The anwer is, that the public are very seldom indeed bears. It goes against the grain. Speculation with the public, as a body, is a fair weather game. When the most potent influences are affecting the Stock markets downwards, ordinary people hold aloof. We shall go more into detail with reference to this pecu-

---

* This depends whether it is a bull or a bear market.   H. W R.

liarity farther on. That it is so is a fact, and it is easily accounted for. When you are dealing with a die, a hexagonal body, you know that it must fall on one of its six sides, and that each side to a certainty will have its turn, and therefore a mathematician is able, from there being a limitation set to the risk incurred, to estimate to a fraction what amount a thrower of the die can afford to venture, five times out of six, on the chances of the ace turning up, so that in the long run he will not lose. A game of die-throwing for money, conducted by one of two players upon principles based upon the doctrine of probabilities, and upon conditions to give him a certain profit, can only be continued for a short time, as the absurdity of it becomes speedily evident to the other player, and play ends. Those with whom outside speculators deal in the Stock markets get all the profit also in the long run, much upon the same system that professional bettors on horse-racing always win in the long run by backing the field. In the die-throwing gambling there is no mystery, at least very little for the ordinary understanding. A person of average intelligence who is quite unable to comprehend that it is a mathematical certainty that a die will show the ace upwards, in the long run, one time in six, can be got by simple observations to see that in a great number of throws the ace will have appeared about as often as once in six throws. The fact of his losing his money through betting that it would not be so would, in any case, bring the truth home to him. The case, however, of speculation in the Stock markets is very different. Although so large a proportion of speculators speedily lose their money, a large proportion of them also, when quitting the arena through want of capital to go on with, seem to entertain a strong conviction that money is to be made at it. There is very frequently an impression left that if this and that, and the other, had been done instead of what was done, the result would have been otherwise. They regret that their purse was not longer that they might try again, feeling sure that with such a rich experience they would avoid the mistakes that had landed them losers. The Stock Exchange speculator has an innumerable number of influences arrayed against him, at least one-half of which he never sees at all until, like the sunken snag, which sinks the steamer without any warning, one or other of them wrecks his fortunes before he is aware of his danger.

A speculative operator has a very dangerous basis upon which to lay the foundations of the argument by which he endeavours to justify himself, and it is this. He says to himself: "there are only two ways for a price to move—up and down." At first sight the chances seem to be as much in his favour as against, and he thinks the failure of others to make a profit must have been the result of mistakes made by them, which he will avoid. But does it occur to such an one that if there were any easy and certain method of making money by speculating in stocks everybody who had a little capital would at once commence to speculate? Speculation in the Stock markets has almost irresistible attractions as a mere amusement, quite apart from its being a kind of occupation which is the most luxurious and exciting mode of making money. It must be evident therefore from the comparatively few persons who habitually speculate, that large numbers are simply driven away from the markets through a conviction that such a vocation must end in disaster. The dangers of Stock Exchange speculation are made apparent when, as a species of gambling, it is compared with the games of chance, whose evil effects upon the community have been at last recognised by the abolition of the tables at Hombourg, Ems, Baden Baden, &c. The conductors of the Bank at the Palais Royal were fully alive to the necessity of limiting the stakes, and also as regards the number of persons with whom they would play at once. Governments are stepping in by degrees to suppress gaming houses, and it would have been more to the credit of Germany if the tables at the above-mentioned places had been done away with while the effects of the golden stream from beyond the Rhine were as yet unfelt by the comparatively poor exchequer at Berlin. The interference of a government is shown again by our own legislature having declared that A should not insure the life of B, unless it can be shown that A has some pecuniary interest in B's continuing to live. The law, however, is for the most part evaded. Such systems are therefore looked upon as bad; but because it is difficult for governments to define in Stock Exchange gambling where *bona fide* business ends and the gambling begins, the most injurious of all games of chance is played year after year upon an increasing scale. At the first beginning of prosperity with a comparatively poor community, gambling springs up in these times in stocks and shares. As a result of such operations Vienna went half mad in the first half of 1873, which was followed shortly after by a financial crash and the suicides of certain bankers at Posen. Older communities, which have passed through the only crucible which in this life teaches people that if money is to be made rapidly the process must be attended with a proportionately large risk, are observed, as time goes on, to be less exposed to the headlong financial panics such as that in which the speculation at Vienna lately culminated. Commercial revulsions of one sort or another, and of greater or less violence, will probably occur during all time at intervals, wherever commerce is carried on, but the gradual fashioning of laws with the view to confine the injurious effects of over-speculation and over-trading within limited areas, as for instance the limited liability acts, will more and more render it possible to stand between the dupe and the financial sharper, and also to observe the gathering together for harm of the dangerous influences, so that they may be provided against in time, or checked at an early stage of the disease. Among the operators at younger commercial centres there is a more feverish desire to gain, but the efforts to satisfy it are not kept in check in the same degree as in places where memories of disaster cluster in traditions among the people, and inspire the growth of prudence, almost as if it were an instinct.

Farther on we shall call attention to the way in which an outside speculator on the Stock markets is handicapped with turns, commissions, and contangoes.*

Very few persons, if any, will be found to dispute the statement that speculation on the Stock Exchange is gambling. The highest mathemathical authorities maintain that there are but two conditions

---

* See definitions of these terms, page 20.

under which gambling can be prudently followed as an amusement, viz.: small stakes, and equal play.

The ordinary gambler in the Stock market is no better off, as regards his chance of winning, than a player against a bank, which can only make certain of winning against all comers in the long run by the protection of a mathematical advantage. In the case of a bank established as a gaming-house the initial condition of existence has always been in the long run either bankruptcy to itself, or ruin to the individual players. As the banks have always flourished, the players, in the long run, must always have been losers.

A gaming-bank is an institution with limited means offering to play all who enter; or, in other words, it is limited means against unlimited means.

The Stock Exchange occupies a parallel position to that of the bank, and the operators* in the markets are protected in such a way that the outside player at speculation must in the long run lose, or no one would be found to take up his challenge. It must be obvious that supposing an outside speculator had any advantage when speculation in stocks and shares were first practised, and through such an inequality of terms he was on the average the gainer, experience would soon show the necessity of rectifying such a state of things, and what would be tantamount to the mathematical advantage secured to the gaming-bank would be speedily arrayed against him.

The number of people who play publicly at games of chance is very small compared with the number of people who gamble in mercantile transactions. And

---

* Operators means here, what is called in New York, " Insiders" and members of the Stock Exchange.   H. W. R.

whereas the former are diminishing, partly from compulsion, as in the case of Germany of late, and partly through the more enlightened state of the human understanding as regards the immorality of this kind of amusement, the latter appear to multiply in proportion to the general increase of wealth, the ever enlarging fields in which public securities are dealt in and commercial transactions are negotiated, and also in proportion to the facilities afforded for speculation generally. The latter part of this sentence should, however, be qualified by the remark that the spread of wealth enables younger and less experienced persons to engage in speculation in a larger proportion as compared with the whole community than formerly. The difficulty of living and the ambition not to fall below the standard maintained by the well-to-do, tempt numbers of young men to endeavour to increase their income by speculation. And moreover as regards Stock Exchange speculation it is unfortunately much against the interest of the stock broker to make public the failure of his clients, hence it is seldom that the wholesome warning of publicity deters others from entering the arena.

Outsiders entering upon speculation with professional dealers in the Stock markets make two mistakes on the threshold. Firstly, they commence upon unequal terms, the effects of which adventitious favourable influences have never more than compensated for, in the long run. Secondly, supposing the terms were permitted to be equal, the outsiders' stakes would be too large a proportion of their means. The losses incurred by speculators as a body have always been upon such a scale as to dispose of the theory advocated by some persons that the mere charges of commission, contangoes, and the "turn" are the only obstacles to success.

Now, if the playing of public games of hazard are on the decline from the interference of the State on moral grounds, the question arises: are there any considerations applying to Stock Exchange gambling, which, as a game, raises it above other games of chance, and entitles it to special privileges? Does the outside haphazard speculator stand a better chance as against the Stock Exchange, than a player at *Rouge et noir* against the bank? The answer must be No. Exactly the same considerations apply to commercial speculations as to other games of chance in which no absolute certainty exists. Mathematicians lay it down as a law, that if any possible event which cannot frequently occur in a game of chance, but which is, nevertheless, a part of the nature of the game, if a bet or stake be made upon the recurrence of that event in a proportion to some large gain which it is agreed that event shall secure, then prudence demands that the game shall be often played; and if this be impossible it shall not be played at all. Here we come to the crux of the whole question of Stock Exchange speculation. Unless a speculator, handicapped as we shall show he is to start with, has enough means to enable him to hold out for the arrival of the event, the occurrence of which is absolutely necessary to his keeping above water, he should not speculate at all.*

What is the one event constituting the benefit for

---

* I consider this most important, and maintain that "options enable the operator to hold out for the event, or at least for a long time, especially if the process is once or oftener repeated." H. W. R.

which the speculator operates? it will be asked. The answer is, the greatest fluctuation in the direction favorable to him which may be caused by any one of the many influences that may spring into action at any time. This is part of the mystery which allures people on. If you tell persons who are throwing a die that the six will turn up once in six times in the long run, they can form some estimate of their chance of winning. But until a Stock Exchange speculator has been roughly undeceived, his understanding gets entangled so that what he sees clearly only at first, is what is in his favour, because his first interest is to discover that. What is against him, he disregards until he has discovered it has undermined him, and all goes together.

In cases where the public play against a bank, it is so managed that the bank has a better chance than the players. It is so managed that a considerable succession of losses can be sustained against the good luck of any comer. One side always secures to itself the benefits of *the long run.* The haphazard speculator stands at the same disadvantage as the player against the bank. His position is always relatively inferior. When the balance is nothing, as worked out by the following rule as stated by De Morgan, then the play is equal:—*Multiply each gain or loss by the probability of the event on which it depends; compare the total result of the gains with that of the losses: the balance is the average required, and is known by the name of the mathematical expectation.*"

It must stand to reason that an outside speculator plays upon unequal terms, otherwise it could not be worth the while of the other side to engage him. As well might we expect a man to set up a shop and sell his goods at a loss. Then we come a step farther, and ask if it be any use for a Stock Exchange speculator to operate if the terms be equal? If such numbers of persons find themselves induced, by the estimate they are enabled to form of the chances in their favor, to play on terms more favourable to their antagonists than to themselves, their prospects would seem to be much improved if the terms were made equal. Although the position of the speculator be improved to the extent of the terms being equal, it is absolutely indispensable that the operations be kept open for a considerable time* in order to secure the mathematical expectation which can have no existence except through continuity. With the play in favour of the gambler, he stands no chance even of holding his own, unless he makes sure of being able to continue over such a number of trials, or during such a period of time, as will give him the benefit of an average of the ups as well as the downs of fortune.

As at cards so at Stock Exchange speculation, there must be two kinds of luck, ill-luck and good-luck, as the changes of fortune which are worth while taking account of. A man speculates, gets his turn of good luck and pockets his gain, treating the money as if it were ore from a mine, or something added to the realized wealth of the world, a pure plus as compared with a plus leaving a minus. For every profit made by a speculator, and for every realized profit made by a *bona fide* investor, there must be a corresponding loss. The man who in his turn is a winner, must

---

*Very important.   H. W. R.

also in his turn be a loser, and what he was plus when he won, he must be minus when he loses.

If the manager of gaming-tables secures to himself a mathematical advantage only sufficient to cover the expenses, he will infallibly be ruined at last. It may be in one year or in five, or ten, but ruined he must be. But he provides adequately against this, and in the long run those who play with him must be ruined. So it is with Stock Exchange speculators.

It is the character of negative events to lay less firmly hold of the mind than positive ones. The minds of Stock Exchange speculators are like other people's minds. A speculator will often attribute a certain movement in prices to an influence which happened to be exercised at a particular moment, and he contents himself with the apparent connection of the two, and looks no farther. On another occasion, when operating in the same way, immediately upon the recurrence of the same influence he is bewildered to find prices move in an opposite direction. This comes from being satisfied with any solution which lies on the surface, and chances to catch the eye. It used to be supposed that comets were the cause of hot weather, and the theory was considered to be well founded, because more comets were seen during the summer months than at other seasons of the year. Hot and cloudless weather is most favourable for seeing comets, but they are no more productive of hot weather than is hot weather of them. This circumstance being fixed upon by one class of theorisers, shows how an event which is positive lays hold of the mind of any person who may be interested in certain effects and is in search of the causes. It is of great importance, in endeavouring to connect certain effects with specific causes, to mark carefully two distinct things, first, the occurrence of an event, and, secondly, our observation of it. Many entirely wrong deductions as to the causes of fluctuations in the value of money, and in the prices of Stock Exchange securities, are made from negligence in this respect.

As every rule has its exception, so in speculation are there a few professional experts who succeed at it as a business. What is contained in these pages is not for the expert, who is well able to take care of himself, but for the ordinary haphazard operator. The professional speculator, who has the right sort of head, sufficient capital, patience, perseverance, coolness, and a business-like aptitude for laying down the elaborate machinery that is necessary for mercantile success, may succeed. In the following chapters it is our intention always to make this reservation, and in speaking of the speculator, who must always lose in the long run, we refer to the ordinary run of men, whom we will designate as haphazard speculators.

THE THEORY

OF

STOCK EXCHANGE SPECULATION.

CHAPTER I.

TECHNICAL TERMS EXPLAINED.

THE members of the Stock Exchange are of two descriptions, jobbers and brokers. The jobber* deals in stocks and shares, either as a buyer or seller, at the market prices. The broker deals with the jobber, and is paid a commission by his principal for transacting the business between the two. <small>JOBBERS AND BROKERS</small>

A bull is a speculator who buys for the settlement† with a view of selling at some future date at a higher price, and gaining by the difference. <small>THE BULL.</small>

A bear is a speculator who hopes to gain by the reverse operation. He sells for the settlement, hoping to buy back at a cheaper price, and gain by the difference. <small>THE BEAR.</small>

Contango‡ means continuation charge; for instance: if a bull operator has £2,000 Brighton rail-

---

* This hardly applies to the New York market. The so-called larger operators and traders take here the place of the London jobber.

† The settlement does not exist in the New York market.

‡ Contango is equal to New York carrying charges—in New York so much per cent. per annum, fixed daily; in London a certain sum from one settling day until the next.   H. W. R.

way stock open for the account, of which there are two in a month, one in the middle and one at the end, and the settlement which is to take place, say in the middle of the month, is approaching without the price having advanced as much as he supposed it would at the time when he bought, he wishes to carry over or keep the stock open for another fortnight. For this accommodation he must pay the jobber in the House of whom the stock has been bought, a certain rate per cent. to allow the speculator to continue a bull of the stock, instead of paying the money and taking it off the market. The contango rates depend upon different circumstances. Sometimes, instead of having to pay any contango, a bull will get something paid to him. If the stock is very scarce, and the jobber finds it difficult to deliver to purchasers, he will be glad to carry over a bull account for nothing, and may be he will pay a consideration to postpone delivery for a fortnight.* On the other hand, if the stock is very plentiful when the settling day arrives, if the sellers have been numerous, and the deliveries are large, the jobber will prefer delivering the stock to the bull speculator to continuing it to the next account, because he wants money to pay those who have sent their stock to market. Under these circumstances the contango rate may be $\frac{1}{4}$ per cent. on the money price of £20,000 nominal stock for the fortnight, or it may reach a much higher figure, even exceeding one per cent. for the fortnight, but such a rate is seldom charged.

The contango rates depend very much upon the state of the money market, and hence the fluctuation

---

* Equal here to borrowing stock flat, or even paying for the use of it. H. W. R.

in the price of public securities in sympathy with the rise and fall in the value of money.

It has become more of a custom with bankers to lend money to the Stock Exchange than was the case formerly; one reason being that, through the more enlightened management of the Bank of England of late years, the changes in the rate of discount are made more in obedience to the varying condition of the money market as a whole, as reflected in the Bank return, than was the case in former years, when the directors would come down to the City some Thursday afternoon to put up their terms when there was very little available money left upon which to obtain the increased charge. In other words, the value of money changes more frequently than it used to, and bankers, desiring to act at all times in view of contingencies, find it very convenient to lend their surplus balances for a fortnight upon easily convertible securities with a good margin. Moreover the risks attending bills of exchange are avoided. The contango rates at the settlement may rise suddenly through unexpected demands upon bankers arising out of a bullion drain, and a fall in the foreign exchanges, which compels them to refuse to continue their loans upon stock. Such stock must then be turned out upon the market, and, if there happen simultaneously to be more deliveries than there is stock taken off the market, the contango rates will rule high.

It may be here observed that the contango charge is an item in the cost of speculation which the haphazard operator seldom takes into account at all; yet, if speculation be engaged in upon a large scale, the item of contango charges may become a formidable one, and, when added to the commission charged by the broker, takes so much out of the possible advance in price which may take place in the period of, say, two accounts, or the space of one month, that it requires no great experience to show that the game is not worth the candle, taking one operation with another.

Take a case in point:—A speculator buys £5,000 Turkish 5%, '65 stock at £50, for which he engages to pay £2,500 on the settling day, which is the last of the three account days. He pays ⅛ commission to the broker, or £6 5s. When the settlement arrives, we will suppose he has been very lucky, and has got a rise of ½ per cent. in the price, which is a good advance for a class of stock which investors do not like, but nevertheless is speculated in a good deal. How does the account to be rendered to him stand, with 6 per cent. contango for carrying over the transaction?

Dr.				Cr.		
	£	s.	d.		£	s. d.
5000 Turks. 5% at 50	2500	0	0	5000 Turks. 5% at 50½ 2525	0	0
Commission ⅛%	6	5	0			
Balance	18	15	0			
	2,525	0	0		2,525	0 0

The operation so far is successful, and the speculator, taking courage from his success, awaits a further advance. He is not disappointed, we will suppose, and the stock continues to rise, to give him the favourable start which is so frequently the cause of his future troubles and losses. During the next account the stock gains a further ¼ per cent., and he credits himself mentally with an additional £12 10s. Here is a gain of £37 10s. minus the selling commission, which is generally charged when the stock is not bought and sold in the same account, and also minus the contango. This second commission, which is usually charged when a speculative account is kept open for a month, is frequently left out of the calculation by novices. Supposing, then, towards the close of the second account, there occurs a relapse of ⅜ per cent., making the price really ¾ lower, which is a very reasonable hypothesis, as stocks do not always move in one direction,—how does the account to be rendered at the next settlement stand? We have—

Dr.				Cr.		
	£ s. d.				£ s. d.	
5000 Turks. 5% at 50¼	2525 0 0		By Balance		18 15 0	
Int. 6% 15 days	6 4 6		5000 Turks. 5% at 50⅛			
Commission	6 5 0				2506 5 0	
			Balance		12 9 6	
	2537 9 6				2537 9 6	
To Balance	£12 9 6					

It becomes apparent, in examining this account, the extreme danger the speculator was in just at the period immediately preceding the relapse, and forcibly demonstrates the importance of acting upon the soundest of maxims in "time bargain" operations, which is, *never to refuse a profit*. We have been supposing the speculator to have been "running the stock," as the saying is, for nearly a month, during which period it had been advancing in price. At the same time he had been incurring expense to have the chance of making a profit by such advance. After carrying over the transaction, he had incurred the certain loss in any case of the two commissions and the contango charge, which make together the sum of £18 14s. 6d. It seems almost incredible that, under such circumstances, he should still hold on when he could close with a profit of £18 15s.; instead of which he closes with a loss of £12 9s. 6d., after having commenced to operate with just as reasonable a prospect of a fall of ½ per cent., and another on the top of it of ¼. On the other hand, everything went as well as can ever be expected on a series of operations, and yet he finishes with a loss. The charges, to begin with, kill the profit, to say nothing of the "turns" of the dealers, and the risks of the fluctuations in price.

Backwardation* is the term for the charge paid by the speculator for the fall. The word itself implies that the charge is for holding back a transaction, as directly opposed to that for which a contango is paid. The one is to carry forward, and the other to carry backward. A speculator who sells for the fall, and thereby makes himself a bear, must pay something if he wishes to keep the transaction open; just as the bull must, unless exceptional circumstances are influencing the market. When the settlement arrives, a bear must either deliver what he has sold, or pay the backwardation demanded for postponing delivery; which, in other words, is the price paid for obtaining the stock elsewhere. If the supply of stock should chance to be large, he will find it very easy to continue his bear account, because the stock he has sold is not wanted. Under such circumstances, the position of the bear speculator comes to be the exact antithesis of that in which the bull finds himself at the settlement when the stock he has bought is scarce. In both cases the charges recede until either the trans-

BACKWARDATION.

---

* Backwardation is equal to the paying for the use of borrowed stock at the New York Stock Exchange. H. W. R.

actions are carried over "even,"* that is to say, for nothing, or it may be the speculator receives a consideration. As in all other markets, it is a question of paying or receiving, and the one or the other depends upon the relation which the demand bears to the supply. As we shall have occasion farther on to speak more minutely upon bear speculations, we shall not pursue the subject at any length here; suffice it to say that the public, as speculators, do not understand selling for the fall. It goes against the grain. Speculating at all is associated, in the minds of nearly all people, with fine sunshiny weather, and a settled state of the political atmospheres of one's own and neighbouring states. The time to speculate for the fall is when growling despatches are being exchanged between nations whose prosperity has reached a zenith where nothing more is to be had, except by quarreling; when the exchanges are adversing, and there is a drain of gold setting in, and the biting winds and sleet of chill October fill everybody with pessimist views; when the reports of shipwrecks and hurricanes at sea fill the minds of Oriental merchants with alarm for the safety of their galleons, and there is an uneasy general impression creeping over the public mind that it is perhaps prudent, under the circumstances, to hold less in securities, and to have a larger balance at the bank. Yet, when the very air seems to whisper coming difficulties and disturbances, and the time is ripe for speculating for the fall, such is the weakness of the human character that the opportunity presented is seldom discerned until the return of sunshine, and the blowing over

---

* In New York, "flat."   H. W. R.

of the storm has shown the inutility of being wise after the event.

Speculation by "options" is of all methods of speculating the most prudent, as it is the most sensible, for all parties concerned. It resembles in some degree the lottery-ticket mode of gambling.

OPTIONS. The indefinite mischief that is caused by speculation which allows the operator to incur unlimited risk on credit is prevented by the system of options, inasmuch as a fixed payment must be made by the speculator at the time the option account is opened. There are three kinds of options. First, is the put and call,"* which means to take

THE "PUT AND CALL" OPTION. or to deliver stock at a fixed price at a future date, for which a certain sum is paid on the day the bargain is entered into.

The second is the "put," which means the option of delivering a specified amount of stock

THE "PUT" OPTION. at a fixed date, the price and the day of delivery being agreed upon at the time the money is paid.

The third description of option is the "call," which means an operation exactly the opposite of the "put." It is the option of claiming a specified amount of stock at a future fixed date,

THE "CALL" OPTION. such date, together with the price, to be agreed upon at the time the option money is paid. The sum of money that is paid for options fluctuates in sympathy with the changes in the value of public securities, and also depends upon the amount of business doing. An option may be done from day to day, or from account

---

* Called "straddle" in New York.   H. W. R.

to account. The option money is paid by the principal to the broker at the time the transaction is effected. When the option expires, the person who has paid the money declares whether he buys, sells, or does nothing.*

Years of experience of this mode of speculating have only shown, as with other kinds of speculation, that the option money once paid is hardly ever recovered. We have taken the trouble to inquire of those who have been for as many as thirty years in the markets, and such is their experience.†

The Stock Exchange settling days are in the middle and at the end of each month. Each fortnightly settlement occupies three days; the first is the carrying over or contango day, the second is the name or ticket-day, and the third is the day for paying the differences, or the amount of money for stock or shares to be taken off the market. The settlement in Consols is monthly, and near the commencement. The extent of the business transacted in the Stock markets has been very accurately measured since the establishment of the Clearing House. All transactions being settled by cheques, the increase in the Clearing House totals on a Stock Exchange settling day correctly indicates the amount of money which has passed between buyers and sellers.‡

The Fortnightly Settlement.

Speculation inside the Stock Exchange by mem-

---

*In London all options are for a fixed date; at New York they are generally made so that the option can be exercised at any time during the pending of the contract.

† This may be true in a certain sense, but if options are considered as an insurance feature, it is generally expected and hoped that they may not have to be exercised, and will simply answer the purpose of insurance and margin.

‡This does not apply to the New York market.   H. W. R.

bers of the House does not present many features which entitle it to comment apart from the speculation as it is practised by the public outside. It is natural to suppose that members of the Stock Exchange are better able to operate in stocks and shares, with a view to profit by speculation than the public who, as a rule, are ignorant of the art they endeavour to practise until all they have left is some bitter experience. Those whose daily business it is to be in the Stock markets must of course know that the outside public are always dropping their money, and in this respect the conviction comes nearer home to them that the play is not worth the candle. There are speculators who are members of the Stock Exchange, but we believe it is but a very small minority that troubles itself with speculation as the principal means by which the profits are made. As a rule, it may be laid down that a dealer who goes out of his market to speculate is just as likely to lose his money as an outside haphazard speculator. Each stock, and each description of shares, has its history, and is influenced more or less by special causes, as well as by general causes. Each stock, therefore, requires to be constantly watched, after it has been studied, and its peculiar characteristics well ascertained. When it is said that these stocks and shares are numbered not by tens, or by hundreds, but by thousands, it is easy to understand that no one man can master the special knowledge concerning each, which however every jobber who understands his business should do, within the limit of those in which he usually deals. Consequently, a jobber devotes himself to a few descriptions which circumstances or inclination may cause him to select.

He confines himself to a particular market, where he is to be found; and if he speculates now and then, apart from the necessities of his business, and to satisfy a desire for a little excitement, or because some special view of the course of events encourages him to try his luck, it is, as a rule, in the stocks in which he is accustomed to deal.

It may be of interest to some persons to contrast the terms used in England with those employed by stock-brokers and jobbers across the Atlantic, and we append those in use on the New York Stock Exchange, with explanations. The inventive resource which is so characteristic of the American, crops up in the terms used in their Stock markets, as in the case of the "put and call" option with us, which the Yankee cannot be satisfied with, but must invent the vulgar synonym of "straddles," which is certainly expressive of the pair of operations in one. The mania for getting rich by making short cuts and royal roads engenders apparently an impatience of terms which contain a single syllable or letter that is unnecessary, however hallowed by time, and hence, "put and call" is superseded by "straddles."

*The "put" is a contract by which, during a fixed time, usually thirty days, a seller for a consideration agrees to take from a buyer of a "put" a stock at a given price, generally several per cent below the market value.

---

* In London all options are made at about the current market price, and the premium paid varies with the character of the stock and length of time, while in New York puts, calls, or spreads are generally so much above or below the market price, and the premium consequently much smaller than at London. The only exception here is the "straddle."   H. W. R

The "call" is an operation of a directly opposite nature, being a contract by which for a consideration a seller of a "call" undertakes to deliver to a buyer a certain stock at a given price, generally several per cent. above the market value.

To "put up a margin" signifies to deposit with your brokers a sum of money, as a rule 10 per cent. of the par value of a stock, as security against failure to meet losses.

To buy "long" is the equivalent of our term "bull."

To sell "short" is the equivalent of our term "bear."

To "corner" a stock is to purchase all that can be obtained and make it very scarce, and also more than can be obtained, in order to run the price up, and "roast," as the saying is in the London market, the speculative sellers; but the "cornering," as we understand the meaning of the word, would seem to apply more to the speculative sellers who are "roasted" than to the stock which may be selected for the operation.

"Clique," "pool," or "ring" are less expressive, and in consequence of other associations, are less happy terms than our equivalent syndicate, which in English financial circles can be mistaken for nothing else than a combination of speculative capitalists which is formed either to divide a loan amongst them and unload their portions upon the public as opportunities may occur, or to "wash" a stock up and down, getting what they can out of the unwary public during the operation. Gold "rings" on the other side of the Atlantic, and foreign loan syndicates on this, must by this time almost have had their day. Each new era of prosperity requires and generally witnesses a new set of ingenious devices to throw dust in the eyes of investors, while the new race of Autolycuses are going through all the old tricks.

In London, settlements take place twice a month, but in Broad Street sales are made for either cash or "regular." In the first case purchases have to be settled the same day before 2.15 P.M., and in the second on the following day. Time contracts correspond to our time bargains, and have about the same conditions attaching to them, with the exception that the rate of interest charged, answering to our contango, is generally 6 per cent., unless otherwise stipulated, and is not influenced by a varying standard such as our Bank rate.

The word "shrinkage" for depreciation is a neat term with which the small catalogue may be euphoniously terminated.

CHAPTER II.

THE IMPORTANCE OF SPECIAL KNOWLEDGE REGARDING THE REGULARLY RECURRING CAUSES THAT INFLUENCE THE MARKETS.

IF a speculator has not closely studied the special causes that influence the Stock markets at regularly recurring intervals, he has not learned the alphabet of his business. We shall endeavour to pass in review some of these. First of all, there is the temper of the public. Many persons have puzzled over the causes which will at one time combine to produce activity among buyers of stocks, and at another dead stagnation; and it is a very interesting study, albeit somewhat difficult of correct analysis.

The Temper of the Public.

There are periods of the year when the temper of investors tends to sulkiness, in sympathy with a fall of the mercury. Dull and disagreeable weather, as a rule, adversely affects the Stock markets more or less, according to the extent of counteracting influences. If we take the beginning of a year, in January investors will usually be found in a conservative frame of mind, with which speculators will sympathise as they perceive it; for it may safely be said that unless the public can be calculated upon to follow their lead, it is useless for professional speculators to stir up the markets. In the first

Meteorological Influences.

month of the year capitalists are in more or less of a stay-at-home mood; and now so many buyers of securities live on a line of railway, they take as many holidays as they can well find excuse for.*

A speculator should have a good aneroid barometer, that has a good big indicator, hung up in his hall, and he would not be very far wrong if he were to buy and sell according to the indications given by this instrument that it was going to be good or bad weather. Most people are like any one you may chance to single out of a crowd, from a physical point of view.† The change from fair to foul weather will have the same effect upon a crowd as upon that one man. Foggy, wet, and cheerless weather sends people to their homes with a contented mind, if they feel they can hold their own until the return of sunshine; just as a storm causes navigators to run for a harbour, or seek the nearest shelter from its fury. When buyers keep away from the markets, prices droop with their own weight, and, from the mere absence of any buying at all, will often fall as regards value, out of all proportion to the extent of the sales. Such a period is a very good one to turn round and buy, as there is sure to be a nearly corresponding recovery with a favourable change in the weather.

Unless there are special causes at work, during the first month of the year the Stock markets are

---

* This is not considered so in New York, where we generally expect a so-called "January rise," which, however, sometimes does not come; and also sometimes expect a bear market in the fall of the year, when money is employed to move crops, which, however, also very often disappoints the operator.

† Somewhat superstitious. I have often observed it just the other way, although generally a very dull market is expected during the hot summer months.   H. W. R.

usually as hard and inelastic as the frozen earth outside. At Christmas-time people make up their accounts for the year, and most of them, having gained less than the total pictured by their imagination, are more or less out of humour, and disinclined to enter upon commitments outside the limits of their business proper. At such a period, therefore, a speculator may look for fluctuations which as a rule will not occur. As February creeps on, if circumstances are generally favourable for trade, so that the newspapers can dish up their daily fare with sauces that encourage their readers to look on the future with hopefulness, losses that are written off will begin to assume less harrowing proportions, and the old inclination to launch out will come to the front.* The professional speculative element in the community sniffs this movement on the part of the public with the accuracy of a pointer that has found his bird, and they commence to draw the credulous by fictitious prices, now and then unloading to be ready when the relapse comes, to commence anew when another favourable opportunity offers. As the spring comes in, with its delights and young verdure, and cheering early sun-rays, which draw the notes of the lark and the linnet, the disposition becomes more general to disregard those strict lines of prudence which the bleak winds of autumn and the shorter days of an aging year, mark out so prominently for observation. At a period of the year when spring is merging in early summer, with all its pleasant prospects of pleasure to

---

* This about corresponds with our spring and fall trade, when the newspapers teem with interviews with prominent merchants and bankers
H. W. R.

come, it is quite natural to suppose that a desire should arise to make money, by which everything could be made smooth and delightful during the most enjoyable part of the year. Then again, as the half-year wears on, there are the dividends to look forward to, which is always an inducement to buyers; the great cities are filling with pleasure seekers, the import and export trade with foreign climes is in full activity after the liberation of whole fleets of vessels which have lain frozen up in northern parts during the winter. The young corn is beginning to clothe the naked furrow, and the various fruits of the earth are appearing, which only to read and hear of is to fill the eye with a sense of plenty that half converts a Tory Stock Exchange operator into an ultra-radical speculator. Under fairly favourable circumstances, the course of general business during the first half of the year is more active than during the second six months. The Parliamentary session is in full swing, and large numbers of people congregate in the capital towns of all European states to transact business, no small part of which is the investment of their surplus profits in public securities. When a new year is fairly on its legs, say in March, if war or such like causes do not interfere with the natural course of events, between that month and the end of June, a speculator for the rise should find, on an average, his greatest opportunities. In the London market more especially is it so, on account of the effect produced on the money market by the collection of the revenue, which always keeps the Bank of England's reserve at a comparatively higher figure during the period named, a circumstance of consid-

<small>A FAVOURABLE PERIOD OF THE YEAR.</small>

erable importance. In the first half of the year also there is more floating capital spread out, and more disposition to extend credit to catch the profits that are to be gathered when the nations of the earth are enticed into activity and movement, both for business and pleasure, by genial weather and long days.

As regards some stocks, there will be no need to make a special study of causes which affect the dividend; but this is not the case with railway stocks. A speculator in railway stocks must watch the course of trade, the colonial produce, the Manchester and Liverpool markets, and note the character of the business doing in the great staples of Industry. Upon the profitable nature of these trades depend very much the traffic receipts of railways. A speculator devoting his attention especially to railway stocks will, of course, analyze the reports of the various companies, carefully noting the weekly published traffic receipts. Then, again, there are the northern iron and coal districts, the operations in which affect the price of railway stocks in two ways which are obvious. A speculator who operates solely in railway stocks should be posted from hour to hour in such matters, or he will be assuredly "hung up," as the saying is, with stock on which he has made a loss.

Causes affecting the value of English Railway Stocks.

Whether there be any more rise or not left in public securities as a body after the turn of the half-year,—we are speaking from a bull point of view, as that is the way in which the public, in ninety-nine cases out of a hundred, operate,—we should always recommend a speculator to pack up his traps and go right away, whether he has won or lost on balance. If he has lost, which will probably

The course to pursue at the turn of the half-year.

be the case, there is all the more reason for not continuing, for he is as certain then as the day dawns, to increase it by going in heavily, or "plunging," as it is termed. If he retires from the scene, and permits his nerves to recover, he will return to be "cleaned" out in a more wholesome frame of mind, which will enable him finally to quit such haunts without probably resorting to such desperate measures as might have been adopted, had his coffers been emptied all at once under a July sun.

At all events, the most methodical and prudent speculator, who manages to amuse himself, and by extreme care, like good whist players, leaves off at the end of six months about even, would not dispute the wisdom of closing his book when all the world was going away for their holidays.

As the first half of the year is favourable for the bull speculator, so the second half is more likely to favour the operations of the bear. When people have had their outing and spent their money, they return to business, and to think of the necessity of prudently providing the comforts needful in the chilly autumn and cold winter. Business begins to slacken in many important branches with the approach of that period of the year when the days and nights come to be of equal length all over the earth, except just under the pole. There may be a good deal of money about at such periods, and yet very little investment business going on in the stock markets. It should be remembered that large extra accumulations of money at the great centres very often mean, in fact, generally, an unprofitable state of trade; and when the foreign shipments leave no profit, from the great merchant

Second Half of the Year more Favourable for Bear Operations

princes down through every link in the chain to the labourer at thirty shillings a week, the effect is felt, and there being no profits, there is obviously nothing in the shape of surplus gain to invest. On the contrary, most people wish to sell. In the later months of the year locomotion for nearly all purposes begins to diminish both as regards business and pleasure, which affects the receipts of the railway companies. If there should have been a bountiful harvest, an important favourable influence may thus be exercised; but even as regards this, it has been evident for many years past that the harvest question in England is of comparatively diminishing importance, and there is every prospect that much of the land now under corn will return by degrees to its primitive state, and will pay better as pasture for fattening beasts.*

As we spoke of the Bank of England becoming temporarily rich, by the accumulation of revenue early in the year, so it becomes, as a rule, poor in the autumn. People are getting more used to this ebb and flow in Threadneedle Street, and the trouble it caused when Mr. Lowe first begun experimenting is not now experienced to the same extent; but still it is one of the elements which is disadvantageous, and to be kept in view by the speculator as a regularly recurring adverse influence.

It is, of course, of the last importance to keep a watch over the foreign exchanges, as these are affected more or less at certain periods when the imports and exports of special kinds of produce and manufactures are active.

Other influences which occur with machine-like

---

* Of course, this applies, in a general way, more to the London than to the New York Stock Exchange.   H. W. R.

regularity will be referred to as occasion may require, and we now proceed to go more into detail.

We will take activity among buyers:—It is clear that active buying in any market arises from a strong demand from persons who desire to purchase for reasons known to themselves. A strong *bona fide* demand for securities means that the public is making money, as they do not enter the Stock markets as *bona fide* purchasers, unless they have surplus monies which they desire to invest and put by in the form of savings. Now, a speculator who is watching for an opportunity to buy should keep in view one set of circumstances as favourable to his operations in the same way that a seller should watch for an opposite combination of causes as favourable for speculative sales. A bull speculator should know that his great opportunity occurs after securities generally have been driven down in price by a severe commercial crisis, which has compelled holders of stocks upon a large scale to realize. In other words, when prosperity is beginning to revive after a prolonged stagnation, and the prices of stocks are very low, the bull speculator's great chance occurs. When the great industries of a nation seem to rise as from the grave, and where lifelessness and inactivity ruled before the blows of the hammer resound and the blast furnace roars, a new life springs through the arteries of the commercial system, and the result is a rise in public securities. The solid rise in the price of stocks is that caused by the hard money-buying by a public that is well to do. At such a time the bull speculator should be in the van, for then the golden harvest prepared for his special sickle invites

<small>ACTIVITY AMONG BUYERS.</small>

<small>THE BULL SPECULATOR'S GREAT CHANCE.</small>

the reaper. Every trade gets its turn to a certainty. We will say, during a period of prosperity, a general recovery of the sounder stocks to a level at which they yield on the money invested 4½ per cent. per annum, takes two years from the time the advance had fairly set in. During that two years is the bull speculator's opportunity. If he does not make money then, he never will. Now we come more to the minutiæ: "Any jackass can take a profit, but it requires a devilish clever fellow to cut a loss," is a well-worn expression in the city of London, but there never was a truer one. During the two years of recovery in prices to which we have referred, there will be a great number of small periods of time when the bull speculator should be out of the markets altogether. To decide when those periods are to be is his *pons asinorum*. After he has once realized the importance of having his accounts open ready for the periodical waves to carry him in and land his profit, the difficulty is to get him to realize the importance of keeping out while the water sweeps back, carrying with it the greedy speculators, who were not content to take their profits. After every great rise comes a fall, and the secret of such success as is possible lies in the buyer getting out at or near the top and in again at the bottom. It is obvious that a speculator must watch for the ever-changing circumstances to reveal themselves and act accordingly. We will suppose nothing extraordinary happens, such as a war, famine, or pestilence, but that the influences during the two years are of the ordinary type. There are the settlements. As a fortnightly settlement approaches, prices as a rule move more or less in an

<small>THE GREAT IMPORTANCE OF BEING NOW AND AGAIN ALTOGETHER CLEAR OF THE MARKETS.</small>

opposite direction to that which they have taken for some days previous, the extent being in proportion to the foregoing movement. <small>THE MOVEMENT OF PRICES NEAR THE SETTLEMENTS.</small> For instance, if for the first week of an account prices have fallen heavily for some reason, such as a sharp bullion drain and a sudden rise in the value of money, there will almost to a certainty be a recovery, because a heavy fall is generally occasioned largely by bear speculators, who will begin to buy back as the account approaches, causing a recovery in values. If a speculator, therefore, is out of the markets when a fall is taking place, he is almost sure to make money by buying at the reduced figures as an account approaches.*

Then among minor influences, which are regularly recurring, are the "drawings" attached to most foreign stocks, and to all that have been issued for many years past. When a drawing approaches, other things not being unfavourable, there will probably be some buying for the chance of getting a bond or two drawn, and the price will improve.†

---

* This applies also to the New York market in so far as that after a large bull speculation there will be heavy realizations, and after a bear campaign or attack the covering process will take place.

† This applies to the so-called '' lottery loans.''   H. W. R.

CHAPTER III.

THE RIGHT TEMPERAMENT FOR A PROFESSIONAL SPECULATOR.

A MAN who wins by haphazard speculation, who chances to operate successfully until he has filled his pockets, and retires with his gains from so fascinating an arena, is one in a hundred. Any one who knows anything of Stock Exchange speculation will confirm the statement that, to the ordinary run of men, the game is not worth the candle. There are, however, conditions under which speculation, in a market where ten or fifty thousand pounds can be lost in half-an-hour, may, under given conditions, be systematically practised profitably. First, and most important perhaps of all these conditions, is the temperament of the speculator, upon which we propose to speak in this chapter.

A man who is excitable and easily led away from a set purpose will, if he go deep into speculation, be soon involved in hopeless ruin. A method of proceeding that has been formed by a careful judgment which has provided for all contingencies, once adopted, should be adhered to as a rule. To be able to follow this advice it is necessary that a speculator should possess a coolness that is not affected by the excitement into which others are thrown by unexpected events; that he should cultivate the art of concealing the dissatisfaction felt on sustaining a loss, which is read at once in the face of a nervous or excitable man; and that he should have the power of calling forth emotions which are the opposite of those commonly manifested under given circumstances. In speaking of the conditions under which speculation may be successfully pursued as a business, it must be understood that we are referring to the one man in the hundred—the professional operator—who will frequently in the elaboration of his arrangements find it necessary to be in the markets himself, gaining what advantage he can by personally dealing either as a jobber or a broker. It is obvious that, when a man enters a market with a view to doing business, his object is to transact it upon the most favourable terms for himself. He confronts those who are prepared to deal with him either way, that is, to buy or to sell. According as he "opens" to the dealers, or, in other words, indicates what he wants to do, the dealers will make their prices. If he be a buyer, they will try to get him to pay as high price as possible and *vice versa*. His business therefore, if he be really a buyer, is to try to look as if he were a seller. He may enter the market under a variety of influences. He may know from private sources, for certain, that a stock is about to improve much, and he may intend to buy as much as he can get at a fixed limit as regards price. If he is anxious to operate largely, and possess but a poor control over his countenance, the

Cool-headedness an indispensable condition of success.

probabilities are that he will be read at once, and the market be immediately raised above his limit if he attempt to buy any considerable sum. In the same way, if being a broker, he is instructed to get a client out of a large amount of stock for any particular reason, the suspicion of which he is not able to conconceal, the price will be lowered to him in an instant, unless it be an easy market to deal in, or by chance an opposite influence springs up at the moment to improve the price.

Ninety-nine men out of a hundred when they are made stockbrokers are comparatively young, who make a start for themselves after having been many years clerks. These men are eager for profit, and commence at once to go through a course of training which daily saps from their physical powers the very element upon which a cool temperament rests. The hurry-scurry, wear and tear strain upon the nerves which is involved in running from one client to another for orders, deprives a man by degrees of those qualities, if he ever possessed them, which are indispensable to the professional speculator. A man whose daily bread for his wife and family depends upon the execution of a certain amount of business, must of necessity manifest some degree of eagerness to do the business intrusted to him, and that eagerness keeps up a strain upon the nerves, and through them upon his physical powers, which weakens the capacity of forming very rapidly a correct judgment, and renders the intelligence liable to become confused under circumstances when to lose the head for a moment may involve a certain loss of money. Professional speculators are consequently very seldom men engaged in the business of dealing in stocks and shares for others, as the kind of labour is incompatible with the maintenance of the cool temperament which is necessary to success.

There is nothing like unsystematic speculation to destroy the cool temperament of a man. A loss incurred through hasty ill-matured operations renders him impatient to recover it, which probably leads to its being doubled. If he chance to recover the loss, instead of pausing to reflect upon the surprise created in himself by a result only feverishly hoped for, he goes on blindly tempting fortune, only to experience ups and downs which unsettle his judgment more and more, until he begins to "plunge," when all is soon over. THE USELESSNESS OF HAPHAZARD SPECULATION

Any one who has moved about at all amongst financial experts, and has closely observed them, must have noticed that they seem to be men far above the average as regards penetrative intelligence, appearing to possess that calm precision of judgment, which, as a rule, is only secured by the deliberations of many persons. Men who have amassed a great deal of money, by their own unaided intelligence, have been men of steady accurate foresight, men who have possessed a large capacity of judging what the public will do in the Stock markets under certain circumstances. A great speculator must make it his study to gather into a focus the various effects that are likely to arise under a given transformation of circumstances, analyze them, set one against the other, and calculate out the effect that will be caused when their forces are spent. ACCURATE FORESIGHT.

We will now suppose we are watching the speculator of the cool calculating temperament, and also the excitable man who is always acting on new ideas.

which, he thinks, will occur to no one else until he has made money out of them. The cool man sits quietly down and reasons with himself, and arrives at the conclusion that what is indispensable to him as ground work is, first, some capital, a sum proportioned to the contemplated extent of his operations. Without this to commence with, speculating under any conditions is about as sensible, and about as likely to be followed by the desired result, as attempting to ferry people across a deep stream without the aid of a boat. Secondly, early information is equally necessary from all other markets where the securities are dealt in in which he contemplates speculating. To render such information as far as possible trustworthy, a branch house in the cities where there are important bourses is desirable. These two portions of the machinery are absolutely indispensable, if success in large operations is to be the rule and not the exception; and the man with the cool temperament will probably owe his success as much to the judgment which showed the necessity of these accessories, as to the well and timely directed operations which, based upon them, result in profit.

<small>THE COOL MAN, OR PROFESSIONAL SPECULATOR.</small>

With the necessary capital and machinery duly prepared for instant action when a good opportunity occurs, the cool man plants himself in a prominent position from which he can discern at once the small cloud on the horizon which warns of the coming storm. The telegrams in the daily press, as they rise above such hypothetical horizon, are the harmless or otherwise little clouds which our speculator will scan, making a note of any which may seem to deserve attention

<small>OBSERVANCE OF THE DAILY PUBLISHED TELEGRAMS FROM ABROAD.</small>

for any special reason, on account of the effect they may be calculated to have upon the public mind. Well-conducted journals only admit into their columns telegrams from trusted correspondents, or from the public companies who supply them, and whose interest it is to adopt every precaution against imposition. An important telegram in a high class journal standing on its merits will always produce more or less effect, and it is of much consequence, but in the second rank, in the chain of machinery necessary to insure success for the speculator, that he be posted hourly throughout the day in the telegraphic news which reaches the seat of his operations. Side by side with this telegraphic intelligence which appears in the press, the speculator will receive private telegrams in cipher from his correspondents abroad, and according to his skill and intelligence in reading between the lines of the two, and judging of the probable course of events by their light, will he be able to operate profitably or not.

Pure speculation as a business, the sole object of which is to gain money, is, from the point of view of risk, removed far out of the ordinary path in which men labour for profit. Only a small percentage of men desire, even if they thought they possessed the required exceptional qualities, to gain their living in such a way. Most men reason that life is short, and that to spend it always in an atmosphere of excitement, under circumstances which keep up a constant destructive mental strain, is a mode of gaining money that involves too heavy sacrifices. The speculator who deliberately selects that calling must consequently be a man peculiarly constituted.

He is generally a man of rather singular habits of thought, who thinks it quite legitimate to start a Juggernaut, and drive it over the crowd, if thereby he can do it profitably. Perfectly legitimate processes of working a market with him, would be considered little better than cheating by the ordinary run of men. He employs systematically all sorts of devices for getting the better of others who are ignorant and less sharp in foreseeing events than he. He does not scruple to lay traps, and drive the public into them, by plying them with fictitious telegrams, if he can get them published, and by forming syndicates to "rig" the markets. He partakes, indeed, a good deal of the nature of the bandit, who prepares the way for forcing concession to his demands by firing a volley into the carriage of the traveller to whom he is going to give the choice of his money or his life.

If he intends to buy a large amount of stock, which he knows is going to rise, he throws off the cloak of secrecy when he enters the market to sell, and depresses the price as a preliminary feint, so that the contemplated rigging of the price may be as little encumbered by bulls as possible. When it is known in a market that a great speculator is selling, weak bulls are speedily frightened out, and when he has such an object in view it is his "game" to intimidate with all the force of his prestige and the power of his capital. Such a man must have a concrete hardness of indifference through which nothing can penetrate to his heart. It is as necessary to the success of his operations that he possess no more regard for the feelings or pockets of other people than a

THE SELFISHNESS AND HARDHEARTEDNESS OF THE PROFESSIONAL SPECULATOR.

hungry tiger would for him if he were airing himself unconcernedly in a Bengal jungle. He has a purpose in view, just as a surgeon has when the amputation of a leg has been decided upon. The speculator's sole aim in the operation is the profit, towards which he cuts his way, regardless of the nature of the obstacles to be overcome, just as the knife is plunged into the flesh, severing the arteries, muscles, and sinews that surround the bone which it is the object to reach and saw through.

For a man to tread a path in which he must systematically not only disregard the interest of other people, but deliberately calculate upon the weaknesses of human nature which characterize the crowd, in order to work upon them for his own ends, it is obvious that he must be constituted in a quite exceptional manner, and not in a way that it is at all desirable that others should attempt to imitate. If uninitiated people who enter the arena in which some of the professional speculators flourish, were to spend some months in gathering information and in close observance of the *modus operandi*, so far as they can get to see and hear, many of them would soon be persuaded that they were utterly useless at such work, and would retire, thanking their stars they had been sensible enough to look on at the game before hazarding anything themselves. From the very fact that but few are successful as professional speculators, it can be safely argued that but few are competent to engage in the business at all, even when educated in all the tricks and deceptions necessary as collateral aids to the machinery which we have shown, and shall show more in detail, to be a *sine qua non*. Those qualities which have, more particularly in the past, characterized the successful diplomatist are also of the utmost importance to the speculator. Successful diplomatists in all times, with few exceptions, have been men who have never scrupled to resort to finessing, chicanery, and the *ruse de guerre* in every form under cover of a saintly innocence that would shame the devil. Deception in all its forms will be found in the armoury of the professional speculator, and the weapons, two-edged, are employed with a laboured precision of which a glimpse by the outsiders is occasionally to be obtained because it is impossible completely to conceal the fringes of the organisation by which his gains are netted.

We now turn to the non-professional speculator, and what a pitiable plight is that in which these gentlemen in ninety-nine cases out of one hundred ultimately find themselves. The members of the Stock Exchange liken their place of gathering in Capel Court to a barn, and themselves to fowls inside it, who repair thither every day to pick up the golden grain thrown in by the public. This description is not exaggerated, and the more marvellous does it become as one reflects upon the subject. Many and many is the man that has toiled and earned a fortune to produce him a competence for the rest of his days, who has been lured into that fatal vortex, in very many cases because industry had become a habit with him, and he found retirement irksome. " I amuse myself with a little jobbing in the stock markets, just to have some object for going up to town twice a week," he says to a friend in the train, with whom he chances to be travelling. Such is the beginning of more sorrow in respectable households than the world has any idea of. Many a pensive

<small>THE NON-PROFESSIONAL OR HAPHAZARD SPECULATOR.</small>

countenance furrowed by the Stock Exchange, carries in its deep lines the index to a heavy volume of lugubrious family history, which, partly from shame, is sealed but to the few who must know its contents. Prosperity brings wealth in its train, and people put by at first their gains, until a taste for the excitement of dabbling in the markets grows into a thirst, and from that into a mania, which is generally the frontier to be repassed with empty moneybags, and a sad heart, by a wiser, if not a better man. It is not so easy to be good on nothing after one has had £5,000 a year, and hence a deal of the mischief that results from the foundering of Stock Exchange speculators.

The haphazard man, who is the antithesis of the professional speculator, will generally be found as differently constituted as are the results of his operations. The man who makes a study and business of speculating, investigating every detail that it seems necessary to probe until he has adapted it to the rest of his machinery, will be found to be a hard-grained man, sailing very close to the wind, while your persistently haphazard man is mostly a person of flabby character, and no less flabby mind, as easily frightened off a line that he has set himself to follow, in the innocence of a heart that expands with a delusive consciousness of possessing power, as a stray rabbit. Such a class of man is to be found by hundreds in the haunts of the Stock markets, and they are always fidgetting in and out, first as little bulls, and then as little bears, disappearing after a sharp panic like flies from a joint of meat that is rudely disturbed by the shop-boy, with the important difference that whereas the flies always get something, the speculators invariably drop their money.

The following letter which appeared in the *Spectator* of the 4th October, 1873, struck us as being *a propos*, as regards a portion of it, of this part of our subject. It affords another instance of the success which follows the trial of a haphazard speculator's "scientific plan." In playing against a public bank the gambler should know in these times that the science of mathematics has been already employed on the side of the managers, and is arrayed against him as a fixed law, working on the side of the *croupier*, whether he wills it or not:—

"A friend of mine who was not with us, but who had had many weeks' experience at Monaco, had communicated a little plan for an all but moral certainty of winning, which was founded on the most scientific principles, but the only defect of which was that the banks gave one no conceivable means of carrying it into practice—a defect, indeed, which I believe he himself had verified by leaving Monaco a loser, in spite of his scientific plan. His idea was this:—It is obvious that even where,—say at roulette,—the chance of the next 'odd' or 'even' is precisely one in two, or one-half, the chance of a run of any *given* eight results in a *specified* order,—such as odd, odd, even, odd, odd, even, even, even,—will be only one in 2 x 2 x 2 x 2 x 2 x 2 x 2 x 2, or one in 256. If, then, my friend bethought himself, you could but steadily stake your money so as to stake it against the arrival of this highly improbable compound event, you would be sure to win. I quite agreed in this extremely sagacious principle, but the difficulty, unfortunately, was in the application of the theory. The bank gives you no chance at all of staking your money against any complex event. It admits only of your staking it in favour of or against the simple elements of this compound event. And, unfortunately, though it always remains highly improbable that any specified run of eight will take place, as you can only stake your money time by time on each single one of the eight component elements of the event, and as, in each of them separately, the chance is one in two, and not one in 256, it is simply impossible by the rules of the game so to play as to have the chances in your favour. I did, indeed, think of requesting the bank to let me stake on the result of two or three successive twirls of the roulette table, instead of on one at a time, but since my French was extremely bad, hardly adequate to protesting against the accidental raking up of my money when I had actually won, and since, had it been better, I had no hope that the authorities would comply with a request so very unsafe for themselves,—the drift of which, indeed, the croupiers might hardly have caught at the first suggestion, but would certainly have suspected,— I reluctantly abandoned my friend's scientific receipt for winning, and was contented to lose.

"The gamblers of our party were but three in number, and all firm of purpose not to exceed the small risk we had prescribed for ourselves of 125 francs each. I was the eldest and rashest of the three, my money being soonest gone, though not for two or three hours, and it was never for a moment doubtful but that I should be a loser in the end. My companions were both cooler and cannier in their play. They did not, like me, precipitately put down their money before the croupiers had raked up the stakes lost by the previous catastrophe. They did not stretch over other players so awkwardly as I did,—indeed, the croupiers had to rebuke me mildly, by begging me to use a rake; and then, when I did use the rake, I managed to knock the most desperate gambler in the room about the head with it, and draw forth a fierce remonstrance, which made me recall with uncomfortable vividness that there was a pistol-practising ground ('Tir-au pistolet') in the garden of the hotel, which would readily furnish the instruments for a meeting, wherein I should hardly have come off with a mere moral lesson. Indeed, I felt clear, after watching my companions,—one of them a shrewd counsel, learned in the law, the other a cool, sagacious Cantab, who came out high in the Tripos the other day,—that neither of them had the true gambling instinct as strongly as I, though so far as their experience went, it seemed to confirm my own. And what was that experience? This chiefly,—that I was distinctly conscious of partially attributing to some defect or stupidity in my own mind every venture on an issue that proved a failure; that I groped about within me for something in me like an anticipation or warning (which, of course, was not to be found) of what the next event was to be, and generally hit upon some vague impulse in my own mind which determined me; that whenever I succeeded, I raked up my gains with a half-impression that I had been a clever fellow, and had made a judicious stake, just as if I had really moved a skilful move at chess; and that when I failed, I thought to myself, 'Ah, I knew all the time I was going wrong in selecting that number, and yet I was fool enough to stick to it,' which, of course was a pure illusion, for all that I did really know was that the chance was even, or much more than even, against me. But this illusion followed me throughout. I had a sense of *deserving* success when I succeeded, and of having failed through my own wilfulness, or wrong-headed caprice of choice, when I failed. When, as not unfrequently happened, I put a coin on the corner between four numbers, receiving eight times my stake if any of the four numbers turned up, I was conscious of an honest glow of self-applause. I could see the same flickering impressions around me. One man, who was a great winner, evidently thought exceedingly well of his own sagacity of head, and others also, for they were very apt to follow his lead as to stakes, and looked upon him with a sort of temporary and provisional, though purely intellectual respect. But what quite convinced me of the strength of this curious fallacy of the mind, was that when I heard that the youngest of my companions had actually come off a slight winner, having at the last moment retrieved his previous losses by putting his sole remaining two-franc-piece out of a hundred and twenty-five francs he was willing to risk, on the number which represented his age, and gained in consequence thirty-two times his stake, my respect for his shrewdness distinctly rose, and I became sensible of obscure self-reproaches for not having made use of like arbitrary reasons for the selection of the various numbers on which I had staked my money during the period of my own play. It was true that there was no number high enough, sad to say, for that which would have represented my own age, so that I could not have staked on that,—but then, why not have selected numbers whereon to stake that had some real relation to my own life, the day of the month which gave me birth, or the number of the abode in which I work in town? Evidently, in spite of the clearest understanding of the chances of the game, the moral fallacy which attributes luck or ill-luck to something of capacity or gift, or incapacity and deficiency, in the individual player, must be profoundly ingrained in us. I am convinced that the shadow of merit and demerit is thrown by the mind over multitudes of actions which have no more possibility of either wisdom or folly in them than—granted, of course, the folly of gambling at all—the selection of the particular chance on which you win or lose. When you win at one time, and lose at another, the mind is almost unable to realize steadily that there was no reason accessible to yourself *why* you won and *why* you lost. And so you invent—what you know perfectly well to be a fiction—the conception of some sort of inward divining rod which guided you right when you used it properly, and failed only because you did not attend adequately to its indications.

"Such is the experience which I carried away with me from amidst the objectionable smells, the unsavoury company, the malignant gnats, the haggard revelry, and the general moral squalor of Saxon-les-Bains; and when my wife reproached me, with triumphant references to her own warnings, for the missing five pounds, I replied, what I really feel,—though I know I shall never convince her of it,—that my experience was not dearly bought. Is it the only case in which the fiction that we ourselves have *earned*—whether good or evil fortune—forces itself with absurd tenacity upon us? Luther himself could hardly have desired a better proof than this of the pranks which the imagination plays us when dealing with that sense of merit and demerit, so closely bound up with our human egotism. We give ourselves credit, and get credit, I suspect, for a vast deal more both of wisdom and folly in life than we deserve. Are nine-tenths of the prizes and the blanks of life at all more ascribable to any fine selective purpose or deficiency thereof in him who draws them, than my losses, or my friend the Cantab's sudden retrieval of his loss? . Yet I still look upon that able and thoughtful youth with a deep sense of respect for his cleverness in retrieving his losses, and on myself with a melancholy consciousness that, like 'Traddles' in 'David Copperfield,' my native awkwardness of mind must have been the cause of my very moderate reverses.—I am, Sir, &c.,

"An Instructed Gambler."*

The Misfortune of Early Gains.

The greatest misfortune that can happen to the haphazard speculator is for him to make money the first two or three " accounts." He will, in such a case, in the first place believe himself to possess some uncommon luck, or a

---

* Letter to "*Spectator*," of October 4th, 1873, Saxon-les-Bains: a Study in the Psychology of Gambling.

shrewdness for selecting a security that was about to move in the direction he had reckoned upon. The operations of the most stupid speculator are fre- frequently attended with such results, just as they might also be on his first essay at pitch-and-toss. Such incipient luck, by drawing forth the commend- ations of others, especially of the brokers—who do not generally err on the side of warning the indi- vidual against the dangers which beset such a path —builds up in him a false estimate of his powers. Early success associates his mind with the gains and not with the losses, and the latter are incurred subse- quently with a light heart, as a sort of accident that will be sponged out by the results of the next throw.

A case came under our notice of the extreme danger of good luck attending a first operation, but it was in another market. A Spaniard had settled in London with his wife and family, and had entered into part- nership with another gentleman. Much money had been made in iron, and prices had attained to an un- precedented figure (it was in 1872). He bought on pure speculation 30,000 tons, and cleared £6,000 profit. Elated with such success, his next operation was a purchase of 40,000 tons. The price fell £1 a ton. He lost all his own and his partner's money, and fled from the country leaving his family desti- tute.

But when two or three losses have been incurred the confidence becomes somewhat shaken, especially after a large operation has been attempted, so as to recover the losses on several smaller ones at one *coup*, and has failed. Then some sort of a system will be tried, but the bad judgment which has landed the haphazard speculator so far without his having perceived the necessity of machinery and a system, will prevent his adhering to any set purpose. Such a man acts on this information and on that, led away by the plausibility of a wiser head possessed by a person who goes about like a big fish in the deep waters, disposing of the smaller fry for his own purposes.

To dig to the bottom of the question without attempting further to widen it, what are the chances against the haphazard speculator? If we ask ourselves whether we have known personally any individuals who have succeeded as haphazard speculators, we must reply emphatically in the negative. It occurs to us on making this observation that we have heard of one individual, who may be described as a haphazard speculator who did get clear off with £100,000, and we believe it to be correct. Everything he touched chanced to go the right way until one morning he raised his hat to his friends and the members who were in the markets at the time, and bid them farewell. He was a solitary instance of a man with sufficient strength of character to say to himself, "Thus far shalt thou go and no farther," and he adhered to it. Many had made as much before, but they could never stop until it was all lost again. How is it so little is heard of those who venture and fail, for the practice would be greatly discouraged if the failures always came to light. All concerned are interested in keeping such matters quiet for obvious reasons. The broker *VERY FEW FAILURES MADE PUBLIC* who does the business for the speculator can measure his means pretty well at the outset, and takes care to keep his client informed so that he may persuade him to diminish his commitments if the times are not promising. The business is remunerative enough to make it worth while to run some risk, and as the client will have always something, at least, to meet his losses with, the broker is generally prepared for accidents. The speculator will, for his own sake, keep his misfortunes to himself, and so the new men come on, never knowing how many have gone irretrievably into the gulf before them until they have passed the fatal barrier of actual experience from which, in all but a very few cases, there are *vestigia nulla retrorsum*.

The chances are overwhelmingly against the class of speculator with whom we are now dealing, for the following reasons: He has no money, as a rule, worthy of the name of capital, and consequently if he is caught deep in by any of the thousand and one accidents that may burst like a thunder-clap on the top of the markets any hour of any day in the week, he is unable to "see it out," as the saying goes. Not being able to take his stock off the market, the settling day occurs before a sufficient recovery takes place, and he is done for. Where there is an exposure to such a catastrophe, that may happen at any moment and sweep away the entire fund, it is obvious that the game is not worth the shadow of a candle-end, to say nothing of the substance. Yet this is the common condition of the haphazard speculator. He stands at the edge of a precipice knowing that a puff of wind will blow him over, and that it may come at any moment.

Supposing, for the sake of argument, we put such a possibility of accident out of the question, and imagine the haphazard speculator not to be exposed to the contingency of such a collapse, what do we find in the second rank of chances against him? In the first place his attention, as a rule, will be drawn to a stock by, we will say, its upward movement. He thinks to himself, "That stock has been getting up, why shouldn't I have some of it?" and he buys, allured as are many others who wait to buy of those who have rigged the market up to a certain price, and then send the tip round to buy. The haphazard man thus assists probably the professional and systematic speculator to unload. He has got in at the top, and only sees his mistake by getting out at the bottom. Secondly, he very seldom pauses after having taken the decision to operate, owing to some special circumstance, to reflect upon the minor surroundings which are very necessary to keep in view. What are these? To buy on the eve of a settlement is a mistake, as a rule. In Stock Exchange speculation the exceptions are of the utmost importance, as for instance—When there has been a very sharp fall in the middle of an account, and it is known that the depression has been due to any considerable extent to bear operations, there will nearly always be a recovery on the eve of the account, caused by the bears taking their profits. The converse will also necessitate an operation of an exceptional nature, as when values have been driven up to a high point in an account by the bulls, to sell would be the line to take as the account approached, because the bulls might be reckoned on to take their profits in the same way. As a rule, however, prices tend to droop as the settlement approaches, owing to sales. The haphazard speculator is always very much discouraged when he has to pull up a loss, he should consequently avoid as much as possible incurring it. If he does not keep these important influences in mind, he will assuredly have to pay for the negligence.

Then there is the fatal blunder made by almost every inexperienced speculator, of never being satisfied with a moderate profit. If he buys, and the price rises ⅛, he cannot make up his mind to take it, but must wait for ¾; when it has reached that he must have 1 per cent.; and when that rise has been attained to, he wants another ⅛ or ¼ to cover the commission. Like the dog, in attempting to grasp the shadow of his bone, he loses all. This is of daily occurrence in numerous instances, and is one of the fatal weaknesses bound up in the frailty of human nature, from which only the strongest and coolest temperaments are able to emancipate themselves. Speculators never set sufficient value upon the importance of avoiding a loss: they think only of the profits. As it is with our money affairs when we say, Look after the pence, the pounds will take care of themselves; so it is with speculators, look after the losses, the profits will take care of themselves. " Never refuse a profit," is a golden motto for the speculator, which unhappily few of them in their greediness have the courage to adopt.

[margin note: GREEDINESS INVOLVES LOSS.]

In parting company, for the present, with the haphazard speculator, to whom we have yet more to say worthy of his attention, we would strongly recommend him if he finds it impossible to leave it alone altogether, *to keep his own counsel.* Do not listen to what other people have to recommend. People who are engaged in commerce in all its multifarious ramifications, care only for themselves, and for no other single soul; it is at all times consequently idle to put any other construction upon advice to buy a certain stock, tendered apparently, with the most benevolent motives, than that it

[margin note: KEEPING ONE'S OWN COUNSEL.]

is to serve directly, or indirectly, the purpose of him who recommends the purchase. In business every one is for himself, and, as the saying is, " the devil take the hindmost." A man who takes to speculating, and has not enough stability of character to lay down certain principles for his guidance, to be rigidly adhered to as a rule, or is possessed of an excitable temperament, had better flee from the thought of engaging in so dangerous a vocation, for his ventures will assuredly result in the speedy dissipation of his inheritance, be it large or small.

NOTE.—I made, purposely, no comments on this very interesting and important chapter, and trust all the terms will be as readily understood by the New York speculator as by the London speculator. H. W. R.

CHAPTER IV.

THE INCREASE OF SPECULATION IN STOCKS AND SHARES.

THE excitement which most men feel in gambling in one shape or another leads to its being practised to a very large extent, in spite of legal prohibition and the vigilance of detectives. Public betting houses have been suppressed, and it seems that betting on horse-racing has diminished; while on the continent, as governments have found themselves able to fill the national exchequer in a legitimate manner, Homburg, Baden-Baden, Ems, and the like, are no longer the chosen resort of rouge-et-noir players; but the vice has only broken out in other places, the results of which will be probably far more disastrous at Berlin, Frankfort and Vienna, in their respective Stock markets, as time goes on, than ever followed the play in the gilded saloons at the places mentioned.*

Marginal notes: STOCK EXCHANGE GAMBLING INCREASES IN EUROPE WHILE PUBLIC GAMING HOUSES ARE ON THE DECLINE.

If it be conceded that playing for money, to which end speculation likewise in any other commodity than stocks and shares is simply the means, produces a

---

* In New York we have now any number of " bucket shops," which certainly deserve the name of " gambling hells." H. W. R.

pleasurable sensation in a man, and that very few men do not experience it some time or other, who have the opportunity of calling it forth, the greater number of men whose position enables them to gamble, will probably do it. At every rise and fall in a country's prosperity there is a flow and ebb in the tide of speculation, not only in stocks and shares, but in all markets. We refer now to that class of speculation which is an excrescence of prosperous times. *A merchant's business is at all times more or less of a speculative nature, it cannot be otherwise; but this is very different from the speculation of outsiders in commodities which they know nothing about.* Many persons would, no doubt, think it strange that there should be a feverish speculation sometimes carried on in such an article as pepper. Yet syndicates are occasionally formed for quietly buying up this article, and ascertaining the exact amount in stock, and the probable quantity that will reach the market by ship within a given time. When the syndicate has complete command of the supply, they commence to "rig" the market, or put the price up, then put the public in and let it down again. In the stock markets the *bona fide* operations, as compared with the speculative, are probably as 1 to 20 at most, and in the colonial produce and other markets the proportion is only something more. It may be imagined, therefore, to what an extent the speculative operations in an article like pepper may be carried when it is considered that the weekly deliveries for consumption amount to 250 tons.

SPECULATION AN OUTGROWTH OF PROSPEROUS TIMES

One inevitable evil attending all forms of commercial prosperity is that they are built up in so large a degree upon a basis of unremunerative speculation. Such a foundation only serves as a sufficient support to the superstructure, while the pressure upon it does not pass a certain limit. If, for example, it be accepted as proved that one Stock Exchange transaction in twenty is *bona fide*, it is obvious that when the speculation in those markets shrinks up for the time, which it is sure to do when it has had its run, a number of stock brokers whose business has been established by reason of the increase of speculative operations must fail, unless they have made enough money during the period of unusual activity to be able to live through the period of stagnation that intervenes before the next revival. And after every eommercial revulsion a large number of them do fail, and it is not easy to estimate the mischief that is occasioned by the shock that is communicated to trade and production by the sudden and complete stoppage of these extra streams of expenditure.

<small>COMMERCIAL PROSPERITY UNHEALTHILY FOSTERED BY ILLEGITIMATE SPECULATION</small>

There are great foci whence proceed currents of profit. The currents of profit may be traced to the great seats of the national industries. The money made, for example, by the great cotton and iron manufacturers of this country, distributes itself in a hundred streams from Lancashire and Yorkshire, to keep within the bounds of two counties.* The larger currents flow into the pockets of two classes, those who are very rich, and those who are moderately so; while the smaller streams trickle into the cottages of the labourer and artisan.

<small>THE INFLUENCE OF TRADE PROFITS UPON THE STOCK MARKETS.</small>

---

* To a certain degree the agricultural industry of the United States takes the place of the manufacturing industries in England. Our manufacturing industries, however, are not unworthy of serious consideration.   H. W. R.

The wealthy direct their new gains as they flow in, into the markets for public securities, and the gains of the labourers follow to some extent in the same direction at a slower pace, through the lower middle class, whose profits increase by the augmented consumption of all the primary articles, in which weekly wages are laid out. In both cases the currents of profit starting from the great foci of production, spread, embracing all classes of the community, like the winter's snows gathered in their wealth in the mountain heights, which are loosened by the summer sun to flow over and irrigate the grateful plains below, and are again gathered up to a large extent for distribution through the Stock Exchanges of Europe.

When this volume of profit begins to be felt in the Stock markets, the harvest time for the professional speculator commences, and with the increase in the amount of the profits of the nation the number of securities increases also. The public securities quoted in the bourses of Europe at the present time amount to thousands of millions sterling more than existed a quarter of a century ago. Side by side with this increase in Stocks and Shares has the speculation in them increased also. Such has been the growth, indeed, of speculation that several joint stock companies have been formed, which are nothing more nor less than syndicates of speculators who have invited the public to join them in buying up a number of securities and making a profit by selling them at enhanced values. A few skilful Stock Exchange practitioners at the head of these concerns have, in many instances, made an excellent business out of the operations, by systematically raising the

An Increase in the Amount of Trade Profits realised, causes an Increase in the Number of Securities

necessary capital and taking the securities off the market, which practically illustrates in broad daylight the legitimate method by which speculation may be pursued as a business, as we have already stated in Chapter III.

The fact of speculation having come to be practised by established companies, where before it was a kind of business that it was considered necessary to pursue as secretly as possible, proves how strong is the tendency of the age in which we live to make royal roads to wealth.*

<small>SPECULATION BY ESTABLISHED COMPANIES.</small>

Speculation, as we know it in our time, is a very different affair from what it was fifty, and even thirty, years ago. Value in all markets in our day is unsettled with the lightning flash that laughs at the bed of the Atlantic as no better than a span of space, while the forces that close in on all sides, representing demand and supply, with a responsive thunderclap, adjust the new level as each market grasps in a moment the cause of the disturbance.

One of the great evils which follow upon the increase of speculation is the demoralisation it brings in its train. Money easily made is very often as easily lost, after which it is difficult to rekindle that healthy desire to work which is fostered by the acquirement of moderately increasing gains through close application to business. Money that cost but little trouble to procure is generally carelessly spent, which, as a rule, does more harm than good to him that gained it.

<small>THE DEMORALISATION CAUSED BY TEMPORARY SUCCESS.</small>

The commencement of a new era in speculation dates from November 13th, 1851, when a telegraph

---

* I do not think that this has been done yet in this country, principally because the necessary charter cannot be obtained, unless companies similar to the Oregon Transcontinental may be classed as such.   H. W. R.

cable was successfully laid across the straits of Dover, and the opening and closing prices of the funds in Paris were known at the London Stock Exchange within business hours. From that day one European bourse after another has joined hands, and the political shock which affects one market, henceforth acts through the electric wires, more or less upon all, according to the extent to which the same securities are dealt in at different cities. The New Era in Speculation.

Side by side with the acquirement of means by the masses of those European states which up to a comparatively recent date have been poor, has speculation as a business grown, and it has been making rapid strides from the breaking out of the civil war in America, when the augmented price of cotton laid the foundations for the manufacture of this staple in parts of Austria and Prussia, where it has taken root, and according to all accounts flourishes in successful competition as regards certain descriptions of cotton fabrics with the mills of Lancashire. New seats of production have been created, and new currents of profit have found for themselves centres for investment. The sharp little panic which broke out on the Vienna bourse in April, 1873, was due to the too heavy superstructure of the new, and much too rapid, speculation, reared recklessly upon very slender foundations. There, in a city comparatively innocent of such collapses, might be seen the demoralisation which follows upon hastily and too easily acquired riches. The effect of the financial crash, which was mended up in a few weeks so that a spread of the crisis was for the time arrested, was such, however, upon the nerves of all classes of the community, that the journals had Collapse through Over-Speculation in Austria.

leaders written in such desponding phrases, that readers at a distance from the scene were inclined to believe that the capital of Austria was about forever to be blotted out from the roll of financial centres. Some little sympathetic effect was produced at Berlin, where considerable inflation also existed as a consequence of the activity in commercial affairs, which followed the large war indemnity payments made by France. There is, in fact, on all sides evidence that the speculation not only in stocks and shares, but in all commodities throughout Europe, has been carried on for several years past, on a scale which was temporarily checked by the Franco-German war, far exceeding anything ever known or heard of before.

Trustworthy figures give the best and surest estimate of the increase in the business of the chief Stock markets of Europe, and where we find the stock brokers and jobbers have increased in number we may safely conclude that the business that is transacted in the Stock markets has increased also.*

In the London Stock Exchange we find the number of stock brokers and jobbers has increased as follows. We start from the year following the great collapse of 1866, when the ranks were perhaps somewhat thinned:

INCREASE IN THE NUMBER OF MEMBERS OF THE LONDON STOCK EXCHANGE.

The number of Members of the London Stock Exchange in 1867 was .. 1,261
Ditto .. 1868 1,297
Ditto .. 1869 1,356
Ditto .. 1870 1,433
Ditto .. 1871 1,442
Ditto .. 1872 1,620
Ditto .. 1873 1,706

* The generally large increase in speculation in the United States and all the incidents connected therewith are too well known, and too fresh in the minds of the reader, to need enumeration here.   H. W. R.

The number of members has increased as follows: From 1867 to 1868, an increase of 36; from 1868 to 1869, of 59; from 1869 to 1870, of 77; from 1870 to 1871, of 9; the diminished increase during this period being no doubt traceable to the Franco-German war; from 1871 to 1872 an increase of 178; and from 1872 to 1873, of 86. It is evident in the increase from 1871 to 1872 that the intention of many persons to become members during 1870 and 1871 was only postponed until the storm raging on the Continent had passed over. In fact it very soon became apparent from the transfer of business, especially of a financial nature, to London, that as soon as the war was concluded the increase in the London Stock Exchange operations would be larger than would otherwise have been the case, as in fact it turned out, to speak only of the loan operations of France and Prussia. It may with tolerable certainty be argued that new stock brokers and new jobbers in the early part of their career depend very much upon speculative commission business, and the above figures, therefore, afford ample evidence of the increase of speculation in these markets.

What are the further obvious deductions from the large increase of speculation in public securities thus suggested, to confine ourselves to one kind of market? If the business of the Stock markets were reduced within safe and legitimate limits, that is, was confined to operations of a *bona fide* investment nature, it is certain that no more than one-tenth, it might be one-twentieth, of the brokers would be required to execute properly all the orders that come into the markets. It follows, therefore, assuming this estimate to be approximately accurate, in the first place that the number of really sound stock brokers, who have a steady legitimate business, upon which pure speculation is an excrescence not particularly encouraged or liked, is small compared with the entire body; secondly, that by far the greater number depend very much for their means of support upon purely speculative " time bargains;" and thirdly, that a crying evil of the whole system is that speculators encourage the establishment of new brokers, who when established are very often compelled, perhaps against their inclination, to encourage in their turn gambling, or there would soon be an end of them. It is thus evident that a large proportion of the brokers in all markets where speculation is carried on to a large extent, must be always living on the crust of a volcano, in imminent peril of destruction from the moment the tide of prosperity, which carried them into their apparently secure and prosperous position, begins to turn.

CHAPTER V.

MODERN INFLUENCES UPON THE MARKETS.

UNLESS a speculator, whether in the Stock markets or any other market, is prepared to lay down all the elaborate machinery, without which, in these times, it is utterly hopeless to attempt to achieve favourable results in any degree, he must inevitably in the long run lose his money.*

The times are very much changed since the head of a great financial establishment, long since gone to his rest, set sail from the shores of France as soon as he was well assured that Wellington was overpowering the legions of Napoleon in 1815, hastened to London, and bought up all the Consols he could lay his hands on, and thereby realised a considerable fortune for himself and his heirs at one *coup*. Here is a memorable case in point as illustrating the necessity of laying down a systematic plan of operations and by sheer hard work, and at the risk of life and limb, carrying it out

<small>A FIXED LINE OF ACTION.</small>

<small>* This is now generally done for the customer by his broker, who endeavors to collect, as far as possible, reliable information and statistics for the benefit of his clients."   H. W. R.</small>

to a successful issue. The ordinary speculator is not to be found with these qualities of dogged perseverance in elaborating a plan of operations, and keeping to strict principles of action from the outset, never allowing his mind to be diverted from his system except under certain special circumstances, for which a margin has been allowed. The electric wire has changed matters very materially in this respect. There is more ease in these times as regards individual locomotion for the operator who has keenly to watch the fluctuations in all markets; he has silent, but at the same time gigantic forces, at his disposal, which he can exercise in pretty nearly any quarter of the globe where there is need for them; but it cuts both ways—he can make a fortune in an hour, or less time, and lose it with the same rapidity, beyond hope of recall should the second line of judgment condemn the action of the first.

All the markets of the world are regulated to a greater nicety as regards value since the more complete development of railroads and of the telegraph system. Each great article of commerce has its head quarters in its respective country, and value from that point is regulated at all the minor stations where it is dealt in, to use a metaphor, in the same way that the right time is flashed through the electric wire to the principal clocks in England at one o'clock from the Observatory at Greenwich. It is the custom consequently for all the leading metchants and dealers to be supplied by telegram with the prices current of those articles dealt in in all other markets, in which they are mainly interested. To compete with those

Closer uniformity of values in all markets through the development of the telegraph system.

who make a steady profit by buying and selling in obedience to *bona fide* orders, a speculator must at least have his arrangements on a par with the non-speculator, if even then he can expect to hold his own without a still more elaborate and costly system of obtaining information, as his necessary profits can in most cases only be secured by his being in a position to anticipate a coming change. A Speculator cannot hope to succeed in any degree unless his arrangements are as complete as those of a man engaged in Bona Fide Business.

Whatever be the operations of speculators who employ little or no capital of their own, or the nature of the transactions of those who risk what they have belonging to them by consigning goods of various descriptions to distant markets in the future, there can never be the same gluts that have characterized the trading of former times. It would, indeed, seem that the commerce of the world must by degrees be carried on more and more by a smaller number of powerful merchants, relatively to the increase of populations and the growth of commerce, and less and less by a greater number of small weak houses. The nature of the system which is growing up under the new order of things will preclude from serious competition any but those who can afford from the commencement to start upon somewhat the same principles of action as those who already carry on and regulate the trade of the world. What chance, for instance, can a man have who starts in the Manchester goods trade, with a view to shipments to the great foreign and colonial markets, unless he can be in a position, by means of his telegraphic information from all the necessary quarters, not only to avoid sending from Manchester, goods The Diminution of Gluts in all Markets. Modern Conditions render it more difficult than formerly for Small Mercantile Houses to succeed.

to any particular quarter where the market is unfavourable, but also to divert a shipment already on the passage from its intended destination to some other point where, in the meantime, prices have risen?

As the system by which the interchange of commodities is effected becomes more and more perfected, and as the division of labour settles itself down into a well-defined science by the good and skilful workmen concentrating their efforts, and by the bad and unfit labourers being forced to abandon what they are unsuited for, so will the demand for all the great luxuries and necessities of life be supplied more completely on the joint stock principle. We see this in all directions growing up under our eyes. Wherever a large demand exists for any service, such, for instance, as transport, or for any article of use or consumption, there will the means of supplying both be organized. We have seen it in armies, in fleets, and in the government of countries for centuries; and we have been watching it for forty years in, perhaps, the most astonishing instance there is, viz., in railways. Formerly everybody drove in his own coach about the country, now nobody does. We have seen it for years past in banking, which, from the nature of the business, would be the most easily reformed upon the joint stock principle. It has also been working and making inroads upon commercial houses with a force which in the end will be irresistible, and which from year to year makes it more difficult for small firms with small capitals, to hold their own against the larger organisations, just as it is out of the question for any private person now to start a bank.

The incalculable mischief that is caused in commercial affairs at certain periods, arises for the most part from the operations of comparatively small houses, which have insufficient capital to enable them to lay down the necessary machinery for duly informing themselves upon all the needful points about which they should be accurately posted with untiring continuity. In a great commercial city a thoroughly experienced banker or money-lender can say very nearly by heart the names of the merchant houses who are known to be beyond all question good for any amount for which they may write their signature. Starting from this nucleus, circles may be drawn defining the various degrees of credit which may be allowed to commercial houses, until a supposed outermost and largest ring of all is reached, which includes the shaky, struggling, poor establishments. Those whose knowledge and experience in such matters is very great could so classify all traders. Now, it must be evident that when the chaos which follows a violent commercial revulsion begins to be transformed into order, the business which the withdrawal of confidence is sure to throw as much as possible upon the centre or nucleus of firms which are comparatively unaffected by any revulsion, will commence gradually to work outwards again, overflowing ring after ring of the supposed lines which we suggest as defining the degrees of stability. This ebb and flow of the tide of credit, so to speak, is the result of competition, and of the fluctuations in commercial affairs, and must always recur with greater or less force and rapidity. It is an automatic working

Every Commercial Revulsion destroys Houses of a Speculative Character, and throws the Good Business into the Hands of the Large, Sound Establishments.

of the laws of commercial affairs which characterizes all markets. As the nature of a large proportion of mercantile business must partake more and more of the speculative character to keep pace with the keener competition of greater capitals employed by a larger number of first-class firms, so must the machinery requisite for each individual firm under the altered circumstances through which prices are affected in all markets become more elaborate. If this view be correct it would seem to follow that the important business of the world must be more and more settling itself into the hands of large capitalists; and that although new houses in all departments of trade will always be starting in proportion to the aggregate growth of the commerce of the world, the large and strong firms will increase in a greater ratio, and the number of the small ones will tend to diminish.

Before the invention of the telegraph, a house of straw could paint up its name, make a show with a few thousand pounds, and enter into very large commitments for good or for bad, as it might turn out. Shipments to a large extent could be made, and if all turned out well, a house might thus, by a stroke of luck, be established to occupy, perhaps, an eminent position. On the other hand, if the first operations resulted in ruin, it was worth the risk, and a fresh start was made probably somewhere else under a new title. Such instances being multiplied in all the great commercial centres, it is easy to understand how markets could be glutted, prices raised to a fictitious level, and all the links forged into the chain which snaps at once, when the tension upon credit has gone beyond a certain point. Matters however are changed in this respect, and are changing from day to day. So small is the expense of obtaining information, compared with the risk of signing a contract with a house of straw, or of doubtful respectability, that the electric wire serves accurately enough for the purpose of ascertaining the position of a new customer who may present himself at a large establishment to do business. A most salutary effect is thus in process of being worked out. The great thing in commercial affairs is to keep out the weak speculative element, and to drive them into subordinate positions to work their way up in a legitimate manner, to become principals. The means of obtaining information now is so considerable, that if a man signally fails, almost the only hope for him is to change his name. In some instances this has been done, and followed by astonishing success, although the way it was achieved would, perhaps, hardly bear close investigation.

So far, we have referred more particularly to the altered character of modern influences upon commercial markets, and we have done so because the changed conditions which affect the value of one commodity in the markets of the world more or less affect all; but, as we are specially writing with reference to Stock markets, we only propose to touch upon other markets in passing.

The net work of telegraphic communication, in Europe at least, is now, in the year 1874, so far complete that, when a pressure of business is felt by the sub-marine telegraphic companies, the complaints of delay are not frequent. The long wires are also multiplying rapidly. The progress that has been made in telegraphy was made known to many for the first time by the circumstances being published, that the Shah of Persia's first minister at Teheran was aroused out of his sleep early one morning, during the visit of his royal master to England, to reply to a message which, to the minister's astonishment, he discovered had a few minutes previously been dispatched by Dr. Siemens, an operator who had been expressly established for the use of the Shah in Buckingham Palace.

<small>THE EXTENSION OF LONG WIRE TELEGRAPHY.</small>

We are of opinion that the complete communication that is now established between the commercial and monetary markets of Europe will tend gradually, if not rapidly, which is very probable, to diminish the effects of what we understand by commercial crises. The opinion embodied in this sentence which was written before the American financial crisis of 1873 broke out, has been corroborated by the great assistance afforded by the Atlantic cable in mitigating the immediate effects of the first symptoms upon the public mind, and in at once confining the disorder within limits which would probably have been impossible in the absence of telegraphic communication. The main reason why we have suffered from monetary panics so severely during the first three quarters of the present century has been from the absence of rapid communication with other monetary and commercial centres, as well as from the absence of large auxiliary monetary centres holding a good average supply of cash, to be lent out on good security to the highest bidder for the time. The facilities which now exist for applying the overplus of grain at one centre of population to satisfy the deficiency at another, has done away with famines.

<small>MONEY FAMINES SHOULD HENCEFORTH BE AS IMPROBABLE OF OCCURRENCE AS CORN FAMINES.</small>

The late exception of Persia proves the rule. Corn is a commodity, and money is a commodity. What applies to one, as regards demand and supply, applies also to the other. A strange nervousness still exists in some quarters about the amount of the Bank reserve, fears being entertained that it will be found too small when the time of pressure comes. Persons who are so loud in their protests at reductions in the Bank rate can never have been buyers of money themselves, or, in other words, sellers of bills. To keep the value of money the smallest fraction above what is actually necessary at the time, by the capricious exercise of a brief authority, is to commit an act of unwarrantable injustice, and to rob the needy. We say if the Bank directors maintain a higher rate of discount than is necessary, they rob the needy, and compel holders of bills to pay an illegitimately high rate of discount. It is urged in defence of this nervousness, that the attractive power of a higher rate is slow, and that the till may be exhausted before the required supply arrives. As and when it may be necessary the Bank should raise or lower its rate, maintaining a reserve which is sufficient at all times if it be about one-third of the liabilities. To speculate upon the future, is to attempt to discount influences which may never be felt. To maintain for a day a higher rate than is necessary, is to tax the public for private ends, to reinstate Protection, and to disregard sound economic principles. To illustrate what we mean, take the case of bread famines. Almost the only nation that has suffered from the worst kind of bread famine of late years, has been one altogether outside the pale of civilization. At the period referred to, the telegraph was only seen in Persia, because it was necessary to use the territory for putting up telegraph-poles to carry a through wire to India. As we write, there is not a steam-whistle to be heard in that country, which is somewhat astonishing, considering that it is so near to us and that it is twice as big as France; although it must be said, in justice to His Majesty the Shah, that he has already seen the benefits to be derived from coming out of his dominions himself, and by letting civilizers in, with *carte blanche* powers, to transform his dominions from a condition, as regards production, which may well shame the representative of an ancient line of kings. With the exception of countries situated as Persia is, with reference to obtaining supplies from other nations, no considerable centre of population need suffer from bread famine in our time, unless under circumstances which no human foresight can prevent. This very important fact was recognized when the first great foreign railway loans were offered for subscription in England. It was seen that by enabling Russia to make railways from the great corn-growing districts of her Baltic provinces to ports to which vessels could gain access during the winter, we should, in case of need, be able to supply ourselves from this source. We have not yet had special occasion to prove the inestimable value of those lines of railway, but one thing is quite certain that, whatever some authorities may say as to the impolicy of lending largely to foreign powers to assist them in constructing strategic railways, for reasons beyond the one given, England never made a better business than by lending Russia some of her

<small>ADVANTAGES DERIVED FROM OPENING UP COMMUNICATIONS WITH THE CORN-GROWING PROVINCES OF RUSSIA.</small>

surplus capital.   Whether or not we have now lent sufficient is another matter.

A hunger crisis arises from a scarcity of bread, and a monetary crisis from a scarcity of money, or what represents it perhaps too largely at some centres, credit.   There are stores of corn kept in larger or smaller quantities by all civilized nations, and famines have arisen in former times, not only from the absence of sufficiently rapid communication making the surplus supply of one centre available for the deficiency of another, but from the failure of production. It is tolerably certain, however, that at all times while human beings have existed there has always been enough food grown for every living creature, if it could have been distributed according to the varying wants of different populations.   Now that this can be effectually done, famines are unknown except in lands whose people are such lie-a-bed tories that they prefer to sit in the sackcloth and ashes of barbarism and want, to humanising the body and soul by the regenerating influence of modern civilization.

Money is as much a necessity as bread in the world.   Indeed, it is of more; for bread alone carries a man a very little way, according to modern notions, whereas money is the lever that lifts every obstacle from the path.   It would seem quite reasonable, therefore, to infer that when the same means have been established for making the surplus at one monetary centre available to supply the deficiency at another, with the rapidity which is proportioned to the more sudden pecuniary requirements that are developed than is the case with corn, the very serious and prolonged disturbances which have been experienced in the past from such a cause would gradually be prevented in the future.

Apart from the single question of rapid telegraphic communication, there is another matter deserving of as much consideration, which is the increase in the number of large monetary and commercial centres.

The Growth of Wealthy Monetary Centres. Of late years the growth of wealthy centres has been rapid, and the reservoirs of unemployed money have thus been increased so that a deficiency at one could be supplied from another at a price. Diseases of the body break out here and there in the world at different periods, and other centres of population get warning, and by quarantine and strict sanitary measures, its spread, as in the case of cholera, is checked. Speculation is a disease of the mind, and like diseases of the body which arise from indulgence, carelessness, and neglect, it in the same way comes to a crisis at places where greed of money, folly, and commercial debauchery hurry people into extravagances and luxury that are sure to result in a general eruption. The growing wealth of continental states is an important feature in the altering character of Europe, from a financial point of view, as we near the last quarter of the nineteenth century. As monetary centres, both Berlin and Vienna have been taking a much more prominent part since the Franco-German war than there was any prospect of their doing before the transfer of so much wealth to Germany by the war indemnity payments. At the same time, London has risen higher, and to a level of still greater importance even than she had occupied before as a trade centre. In proportion as other such centres are growing in influence with their reserves of floating capital and credit is Londen shored-up, so to speak, against the violence of a commercial crisis by the growth of subsidiary monetary centres, which form the second line of defence. Such a second line of defence against a sudden collapse of credit, such as we have experienced several times during this century, is of the utmost importance to a centre like London, where the existence of an elaborate system of book-credits causes such an economy of the currency.

Among exterior modern influences is the rapidity with which the large professional speculators obtain cipher telegrams, informing them of important events that transpire abroad which are calculated to influence prices in all markets. The effect of the rapidity with which such events are thus made known is that, whatever influence they may be calculated to exercise upon certain values, it will almost always have been discounted before the ordinary haphazard speculator gets to know anything about it. Close observers will be able to confirm this by having remarked that all political information is, as a rule, known sooner at the Stock Exchange than anywhere else.* So it is with all news that is likely to affect prices that are quoted in the public prints. Many a man has gone quietly up to the city some morning after studying his newspaper telegrams and bought or sold some stock on speculation, under the impression he was stealing into the enemy's camp while the foe was asleep. On looking closer into the matter—of course when it is too late—he discovers that the in-

Private Cipher Telegrams as Exterior Influences upon Prices.

---

* This also applies to important changes or other matters affecting all kinds of corporate property, &c. . H. W. R.

formation he has been so cunningly operating upon is already, for many hours, perhaps half a day, a matter of history.

What is the altered character of the interior influences? One, and perhaps the most, important, is, that syndicates of powerful speculators act in conjunction with the dealers in the markets. There are distinct markets for certain stocks and certain classes of stocks, and the jobbers confine themselves more or less to dealing in a few descriptions. In a wealthy community there will probably always be a large number who cannot control a restless desire to be operating in the markets, who must now and again try their hands at speculation, as circumstances seem to present favourable opportunities. There are periods in the prosperity of every community when individuals are known to have made profits in their business, and in the natural course of things seek investments for their gains. Securities at such times are created on a great scale to suit the taste and appetite of the public. In the first stages of the creation of new securities considerable profits are made by *bona fide* investors, which in course of time attracts the attention of speculators without means, who think that they have but to venture and they also will gain. After a time inflation sets in ; and we may here ask the speculator if it ever occurs to his mind that unstandings exist between the syndicates of professional speculators and the dealers, whereby the former get to know to what extent the public have bought by seeing the jobbers' books? It is easy to see the power a syndicate with large means may exercise by

<small>THE ALTERED CHARACTER OF INTERIOR INFLUENCES UPON PRICES.</small>

<small>THE CREATION OF SECURITIES TO MEET THE DEMAND</small>

such a system as this, even in a large market, supposing they could get to see the books only of the larger jobbers. We will suppose, for instance, the public can be induced to buy a certain stock largely on some fictitious information. If, at the close of each of three or four days buying for the rise, it was ascertained by an examination of the jobbers' books that accounts were open in a stock to the extent of half a-million of money by over a hundred different purchasers, it becomes evident that there is a tree of ripe fruit grown as it were by magic, and the syndicate has nothing to do but to pluck it. Out of a hundred buyers at least a third would probably rush out and take their loss at the first indication of their being on the wrong scent. One of the great faults which characterises all speculators, with very few exceptions, is that they cannot summon courage to "cut a loss" at once. The object of buying was to gain, and the mind is associated with a profit in connection with a rise on the transaction, and it is very difficult to change about, and gain, in a negative sense, by not losing more. It is upon this weakness of speculators individually, in not being able to "cut a loss," that bands of marble-hearted riggers lure the public into holes, and squeeze their purses before they let them out. With such tenacity do speculators hold on to a stock, hoping for a recovery when they have made a loss, that they will leave it as a man drops into the sea from a burning ship, only when he is singed by the flames. Many speculators on discovering they are on the wrong tack gather themselves up *pour mieux sauter*, and turn round and sell for the fall, believing they shall be quick

<small>GETTING BEHIND THE SCENES.</small>

<small>THE DIFFICULTY OF "CUTTING A LOSS."</small>

enough to catch it and swim with the downward stream before it is spent. In the greater number of cases, such speculators watch the fall far enough to be sure they are right in their view of the way the price is going, and then they "get in." What is the usual result? Hesitation in the second operation has caused them to miss the mark, and the account is closed with a loss on both transactions; the speculator having bought at or near the top, and sold at or near the bottom.

CHAPTER VI.

CACOETHES OPERANDI.

THE bane of nearly all speculators of the soft-grained type—by which we mean men whose will and judgment bends this way and that, like a reed that nods allegiance to any quarter of the world according to the blow of the wind—is, that they are for ever on the itch to do something. There is no getting them to wait for an opportunity. There are two sorts of opportunities, and the distinction between them is important. The speculator feels much more at home in availing himself of one than of the other. The man who can wait for ex- *Waiting for Extremes.* tremes is the one who will have the best chance of making extreme profits, provided he can be fairly sure of a good grasp of the duration of passing influences. One kind of opportunity is after a sharp fall in prices. As we have before remarked, most speculators feel more at ease in operating for the rise, and consequently know best what they are about after a fall in prices, and they make themselves bulls. The other kind is after a well sustained rise. But it has been generally observed that speculators sell bears of stock with more timidity than they buy bulls. One reason, no doubt, beyond that referred to is, that they have a feeling in their own minds that in selling for the fall they are going against the current, which on the surface seems to be a rash proceeding. But in being able to combat this feeling lies one of the main elements of success. It is out of the public that successful speculators make their money, and consequently there must be the greater chance of losing by following the lead of the public. Of the two opportunities therefore of which a speculator can avail himself with the most advantage, that of looking on at a rise and opening a bear account at the new prices is, under ordinary circumstances, the most worth his attention, as the reaction is generally more rapid after a sharp rise than after a fall, owing to there being more new interests engaged in causing it. A rapid rise is promoted largely by speculators whose operations for purposes of enticing the public to buy, may be compared to the exertions of a horse in a great race that is entered to make the running for the favourite. Those speculators are more anxious, as a rule, to realize their profits as bulls, off high figures, than they are to close bear accounts; for, when a panic has driven prices down, some time will elapse before confidence revives, and in the meantime it may be renewed.

REACTION GENERALLY MORE RAPID AFTER A SHARP RISE.

A person who cannot withstand the itching desire to have an interest in something or other, is almost sure to be a man of that soft texture of character that yields to influences that are unworthy of serious attention, and he will consequently be led into error and loss probably oftener than not, and his operations will end in failure. It must be obvious to every reflecting mind, that so dangerous a game as Stock

Exchange speculation, or speculation which partakes of the same nature, in another commodity, entered into, if it be only partly to satisfy a craving for some sort of excitement, is a very unwholesome pastime.*

Of all occupations Stock Exchange Speculation is the last to be thought of as an amusement for the man who wishes for some light kind of business that can be done with an off-hand air, and without any of the drudgery that is the real power in money-making. And yet there is no doubt that a large proportion who feed the ever copiously flowing stream of profits that the members of the Stock Exchange are diligently gathering from day to day, are persons who, having nothing better to do, are drawn by an insatiable desire for some occupation into the ranks of the haphazard speculators. Once fairly entangled in the meshes of loss, the struggles to recover it are usually attended by worse disasters.

It may also be shown that a desire to satisfy a craving for a class of excitement which partakes somewhat of the nature of sober business, in its earlier stages at least, allows admission to the mind of an element which makes havoc with the judgment, and consequently forms an ingredient in the nature of a speculator, which is almost sure to bring him sooner or later to grief. Before a man enters upon the business of speculation, he ought, if he is to have a fair chance, to clear his reasoning powers from any such unwholesome encumbrances as even the faintest desire for excitement. Every step a speculator takes should be, as far as possible, as de-

---

*These remarks apply with the same force, if not more so, to grain, provisions, cotton, petroleum, &c. H. W. R.

liberate as if he knew perfectly well that the slightest miscalculation would certainly involve him in loss.

In engaging in speculative commitments, the great difficulty that presents itself is not so much what to buy or sell, as what not to buy or sell. When to do something, and when to do nothing. Here lies a problem, the solution of which costs such a number of speculators their money and their peace of mind afterwards, to say nothing of the chronic dyspepsia that afflicts them until they are forced to quit the field.

<small>WHAT NOT TO DO.</small>

If the time a man spends in finding out the mistake he has made in selecting this or that stock haphazard for speculative purposes, were devoted to obtaining some special information about one particular stock which he might have good reason for believing was worth attention, his chances of making money would much improve.* This plan is adopted by the more sensible speculators who sufficiently understand the difficulties of the business to recognize the importance of laying down certain principles of action. Money cannot be made for a continuance with any degree of certainty without hard work. When this proposition is demonstrated, which it undoubtedly can be, the whole question of speculation as an occupation, a pastime, or a business, call it what we will, resolves itself into this, that unless a man devotes the same hard work to it that is necessary to earn a fortune in any other calling, plus the possession of an intellect of a special order and considerably above the average, he must be a fool to speculate at all.

<small>SPECIAL INFORMATION</small>

<small>MUCH MONEY ONLY OBTAINABLE AS A CERTAINTY BY HARD WORK.</small>

---

*I think his remark is worthy of serious consideration. H. W. R.

In order to bring more forcibly home to the mind of a man who may know nothing of Stock Exchange matters, the wisdom of imprinting upon his understanding the uselessness, in the long run, of playing at what is nothing better than pitch-and-toss, we will just sketch a case in point as an instance :—Supposing a speculator to enter the office of a stock broker. He has, perhaps, some hazy ideas about the future financial condition of Spain, for example. He has noticed the stock has fallen to 19¾, and this seems to be very low for a country which has so far struggled against the corruption of its rulers, and the laziness and apathy of its population as a body, and has managed for a long time, by hook or by crook, to meet the exterior coupons by paying them in other people's cash. The probabilities certainly must be, he thinks, in favour of their paying another half-year's interest, if after that the deluge of national insolvency should flood the land. He contents himself with gathering to a focus the intelligence that stands from morning to morning in the telegram columns, and comes to the conclusion that something will turn up to supply the exchequer with another loan to meet the next dividend, and in that case the stock must at once jump up to 22 at least, perhaps to 25, as there would then be six months to turn round in. Now, what we submit is, that to speculate deliberately upon such a system as this, is not far removed from insanity; and yet it will be acknowledged by those conversant with the modus operandi of the haphazard speculator, that his plan of attack is based, for the most part, upon this absurd system of guess work, no serious trouble being taken to estimate the extent of the forces opposed.

marginal note: AN AVERAGE INSTANCE OF HAPHAZARD SPECULATION.

Some fanatical faith is placed in the doctrine of chances that the fluctuation wished for will occur, and he shuts his eyes and waits. To sit at home and guess at what the present or future financial condition of any country may be, and to risk your money under such conditions, is worse than reckless.

Supposing, on the other hand, the hypothetical speculator, instead of acting upon the impression made on his mind, by superficial influences, were to start for Spain and take the trouble to get behind the stock, so to speak. In one week, if he occupied a position in life sufficiently high to enable him to get trustworthy information, he would be in a position almost certainly to know whether there was a chance of such an event coming off, as for instance, the next coupon being paid. This would be at least a business-like way of setting out on a speculating expedition, a method of proceeding such as is pursued by a syndicate of speculators who propose to purchase a foreign mining property, for example. A man of sense who buys anything, the value of which depends upon a set of circumstances operating at a distant spot, naturally proceeds thither, or satisfies himself through some trusty agent that such circumstances exist, or that they do not. If he be contented to buy twenty thousand spanish Stock at twenty, on the chances of the power that is, or may be, from one week to another, being able to pay the dividend, because so far they have just managed to do so, he would be deserving of no sympathy if he found himself in a couple of weeks with his stock at 17, and his banker's balance less by six hundred pounds.

The reason why so much money is lost by this loose mode of proceeding is, because haphazard speculation possesses a peculiar charm for certain loose natures, which are roused into a pleasureful excitement by running risks. They defend the viciousness of their lazy amusement by saying to themselves that the chances must at least be as much *for* them as *against* them, inasmuch as there are but two ways for the price to go—up and down. Many a man who has fed and encouraged this itching sensation, which can only be appeased by having passed through the excitement of running a certain risk, finds himself so bound by its spell that in very many cases nothing short of absolute ruin succeeds in quenching his thirst for such excitement.

CHAPTER VII.

THE PIT-FALLS.

THERE are perhaps very few speculators of the haphazard type who take the trouble to find out the extent and power of the hidden forces that are arrayed against them in the markets.

<small>HIDDEN FORCES OPPOSED TO THE SPECULATOR</small>

Every stock, it should be remembered, has either a small or large market to itself. In some stocks it is possible any time of the day to deal at at 1-16 price,* while in others there may be a difference of 1, 2, 3, or even 5 per cent. under certain circumstances, between the buying and the selling price. A speculator operating in a stock in which he can always deal at a close price is able to undo his bargain with only a trifling loss probably, if he finds out at once that he has operated under some misapprehension; but if he has bought a stock the purchase price of which is say 35, and if he wants to sell he can only get 34, he has incurred a loss of 1 per cent., besides the commission, before he can cancel the bargain. This belongs obviously to the alphabet of the business, but the haphazard speculator seldom learns his alphabet until the use of it is no longer of any value.

---

* At the New York Exchange nothing less than ⅛. H. W. R.

A broker, it may be said, should warn his client before putting him into a stock the price of which is wide; but unfortunately such warnings do not increase the number of commissions, and, apart from that, if a speculator does not take the trouble to inform himself accurately upon such a point, placing no reliance upon the advice of any one, he deserves to lose his money. Some markets are so small that a speculator once in, is what is called "roasted" before he is let out again. A particular man very often is the only dealer in the market in a certain stock of which perhaps the supply is also very limited. Under such circumstances a haphazard speculator who may chance to have observed some rather violent fluctuations thinks there is a good opportunity to make some money, and he sells a little bear of a couple of thousand pounds nominal of stock. The round sum, and the channel through which the sale comes, helps the jobber to read the operation. The decoy-duck in the shape of the fluctuations in price, lures two or three more sportsmen on to the dangerous ground, and when they want to get out the price is put up against them, and they are quietly mulcted of £50 each, without a chance of getting even a sight of their enemy, or any value for their money but experience. _{THE "TURN."}

A speculator who consults a not over-scrupulous broker as to the best thing to buy for the rise, runs the risk of taking some stock off the broker's hands that he is desirous to get rid of. It is far better that a broker should not be exposed to such a temptation, and a speculator will do well to make it one of his maxims to put no trust in any one when he is engaged in a business in which it is the _{THE DANGER OF TAKING ADVICE.}

object of everybody with whom he comes in contact to make something out of him.

Supposing a broker is not directly interested in any particular stock when a client who is in doubt what to do consults him; it does not then follow that the client can depend upon getting absolutely disinterested opinions. The broker may have just put some other clients into a certain stock, and with a view to his own advantage, by helping to make money for them, he will lean probably to some extent in the direction of advising others to purchase the same stock.

<small>A DISINTERESTED OPINION.</small>

There is an old saying that it is unadvisable to have all your eggs in one basket, a saw that is constantly quoted among both *bona fide* investors, as well as among speculators. A broker is not desirous that his clients who speculate should be interested very largely in one stock. He prefers to have the liability spread over the market, for obvious reasons. If a client fancies a particular stock, or has good reasons for believing it is about to improve, and he goes to his broker with a view to increase his stake, he will not receive the same encouragement as if he selected something else. The influence thus brought to bear arises from selfish motives, and proves again that the client should keep his own counsel. If he have no decided views himself, it is certain he had better do nothing, for speculation thus entered upon is doubly and childishly haphazard.

<small>ALL THE EGGS IN ONE BASKET.</small>

The more organized methods of speculation which prevail in these times, cause the public to be mulcted of their money in a much more wholesale manner than was the case formerly. They are now driven like sheep, or rather enticed into a pen, and there mercilessly squeezed until they are glad, like some of the players at Homberg have been, to have their third-class fare paid home. A number of brokers or jobbers, or both, in the markets will be instructed to run a stock up, after a goodly number of bears have been decoyed in by a gently falling price from day to day, seasoned with unfavourable reports. Those who are able to command a sight of the jobber's books, know of course exactly the position of affairs, and the price is rigged until the weak speculators for the fall are simply frightened in. This is done upon even a more extensive scale in the opposite direction, for the simple reason that the general public as speculators, are bulls by nature. Bear operations seem to go against the grain of the average man who acquires a first taste for speculation, probably by possessing some amount of stock which improves in price after he has bought. Money thus easily made, as it seems to be, out of nothing, encourages other purchases with a view to resale before the settling day arrives. Thus small figures grow to large ones; and small profits, in frequent atiempts to multiply them, usually end in large losses. A good stock, or the shares of a good company, that has long been discredited from a cause which may be suddenly removed, has frequently been used for literally flaying the public when they have rushed in as bulls. A memorable case in point was the rigging of the shares of the **Erie Railway** Company. Upon the occasion of the assassination of Fisk, jun., the shares were run up and the public enticed in by daily advancing figures far above the actual merits of the shares, from a dividend point of view. Numbers of persons were induced to believe the price would range high from that moment. The quotation subsequently declined, and one by one the unhappy bulls were disgusted into taking their losses, whilst those who had rigged the market were following them down as bears, and making a fine thing out of the affair. The same game was played with the public when Jay Gould was ousted from the presidency of the Company, when the price was run up to $57\frac{1}{2}$, and gradually went back, even as low at one time as to 28, afterwards recovering to about 50. As compared with the professional tricksters who manage these riggings of the markets, even the best of the outside speculators, who have had long experience and think they can stand on one side and profit by the gullibility of the public, discover themselves frequently the wrong way, when the course of the market for some time at length reveals unmistakably the drift of the experts behind the scenes. The man who must speculate should be early in, and early out, being contented with a cut off the loaf and pass it on; for it is the profits missed that ruin the speculator.

[margin: A CASE OF ROASTING THE BULLS.]

[margin: A CUT OFF THE LOAF AND PASS IT ON.]

There is scarcely a more important point to which to draw attention, than that of being contented to watch for an opportunity. It is fatal to the success of a speculator to be always with stock open in the markets. The casual observer must be well aware[*] that now and again a small panic occurs, and the general level of values is knocked down perhaps two, three, or

---

[*] Even such fluctuations are considered as unworthy of consideration in American railroad stocks, where fluctuations of 10 per cent. and even more, within a comparatively short time, are of frequent occurrence.   H. W. R.

on serious occasions as much as four per cent., according to the inflated state of particular stocks at the time. A speculator who has twenty or thirty thousand pounds nominal of stock open at such a time, stands in a moment to lose eight or twelve hundred pounds at a blow. With such a contingency always hanging over him, it must be evident to the prudent man that in order not to expose himself more than he can possibly help to such a catastrophe, which may happen at any moment, he should operate, be contented with a moderate profit, and close.* The obvious advantage of looking on for comparatively long periods, and having commitments for short periods is, that the chances will be much more in favour of the speculator when a panic causes a heavy fall. He is then free to buy at prices which are sure to be unduly depressed, and instead of the dreary waiting to recover from losses incurred, he makes in a very short time probably a handsome profit, again retiring to avoid the reaction that follows a sharp recovery, to await a similar favourable opportunity. To be overtaken, with large amounts of stock open for the rise, by a panic which engulphs a speculator's money and upsets his judgment at the same time, is among the least excusable faults when committed by the man who starts upon any system. The haphazard speculator is almost sure to have accounts open when a panic takes place, because he is, as a rule, in a fever lest he shall miss a rise, and is, therefore, never contented unless he is " in the swim," and hence the severe handling he gets by never seeing the cataract until he is half way to the bottom.

[margin note: SHORT PERIODS IN AND LONG ONES OUT.]

---

* Or through Options at least insure himself against loss.   H. W. R.

CHAPTER VIII.

SPECULATION WITH CAPITAL.

It is in the nature of free trade, that whatever mathematical advantage is to be obtained at all is more accessible to the rich speculator than to the poor one. The rich player consequently can make himself the stronger one, and the operator with capital has advantage over the operator without.* So far, however, as it is worth while to exercise at all the natural skill in Stock Exchange speculation, which one individual may possess beyond another, there can be no doubt that a less rich, but very skilful operator, would very materially, if not quite, in the long run, restore the balance of advantages which was against him at the start. As the haphazard speculator always must enter the lists at a disadvantage or on unequal terms, it follows that the exercise of any amount of skill will only bring him somewhat nearer to, or at best slightly beyond, holding his own; and in that he would fail in the long run. If he lay down all the machinery necessary to success in ordinary business, he virtually passes the limit which de-

_{RESTORING THE BALANCE OF ADVANTAGES.}

---

* In Options, however, the poorer speculator virtually borrows, for a fair consideration, the capital and credit of the rich operator.   H. W. R.

fines pure speculation by reducing the risks to such a minimum that they are no more than the percentage which is an inevitable element in all mercantile transactions.

That it is absolutely necessary that a speculator should possess capital may be illustrated from several points of view, and although we may become, perhaps, tedious by repetition, as in Chapter III., for instance, when speaking of the temperament of a speculator, the time spent in double reflections by the uninitiated may prevent shipwreck, at least in the first stages. A man who is going to operate on a large scale will be equally dishonest if he have not a large capital, as a small speculator who has no more than his £300 a year out of which to save up if he loses more than he can pay. It seems hardly necessary to state that a speculator who operates in the Stock markets and loses without having anything of his own wherewith to pay, inflicts just the same loss upon the broker who does the business for him, as he would upon a butcher of whom he purchased a leg of mutton, consumed it, and then declared he had no money. It is really, however, necessary to make this statement, clear as is the truth of it, because speculators, as a rule, do not realize the liability in the same way. There are differences in degrees of tangibility in these matters, no doubt, and hence the morally injurious effects of speculation and all kinds of gambling. A leg of mutton is a solid substance, and the fact of consuming it not only impresses the circumstance upon the mind, but upon the body too, in the shape of the recollection that the body benefited by the food. By the aid of the remembrance of the benefits

[margin: THE NECESSITY OF SOME CAPITAL.]

that grow out of the consumption of the leg of mutton, the liability to pay for it becomes realizeable in a high degree, and no man allows himself to dream of escaping from it. It is not so in the same degree with a liability incurred by "time bargain" speculation, because what represents exactly the same tangible substance, was never fully, or even partially, realized as such.

All large speculators are well known. If they try to operate through other persons in order to deceive, the truth leaks out some time or other. Large orders are very difficult of execution, unless the broker is either of very good standing himself, or hints at the source from which he receives his instructions. Unless, therefore, it can be shown that the real operator has a very broad pecuniary back, an attempt to buy or sell large amounts of stock through brokers is difficult. It is sometimes necessary to have capital to throw away in feints, before the speculator commences his operations, just as a general may find it expedient to throw away a quantity of amunition, and even the lives of some of his soldiers, to draw off attention from the real attack. A speculator who contracts to bring out a new loan, unless the security he has to offer is of the highest class, runs considerable risk of losing his money, as he has, as a rule, to pay something down to the borrower as a guarantee of good faith, and to allow him also to taste the ready cash, as some immediate consideration for entering upon business, which, if successful, is of all business the most remunerative. This kind of speculation belongs to *la haute finance*.

A supply of ready money is essential to to the speculator in all markets, and it is marvelous that there can be so many persons who have to grope their way by the aid of bitter experience through the thick darkness of their ignorance to such a shining light of truth as this. And the full realization of this truth is, in most cases, only obtained at an expense which renders it impossible to repeat the experiment.

After a severe commercial collapse, like that of 1866 for instance, all securities are low in price, holders of them have been compelled to realize through the *debacle* which has for the time destroyed credit, turned profits into losses, and frightened everybody into hoarding the precious metals. When things are beginning to mend, and a resurrection of industries takes place, the tide of the national profits begins to turn, and, rippling back into innumerable channels where securities of all sorts have laid high and dry and neglected, again floats them into notice. Just as when there is no use for the plough the oxen are idle, so when the great industries of a nation are stagnant, floating capital lies idle, and is cheap. In such times the speculator of good judgment, with ten or twenty thousand pounds can make money without much risk if he is satisfied to watch the general recovery of prices up to a certain level, and then realize. We will suppose money at 3 per cent., and the best English railway stocks some thirty per cent. below the value they will reach when the country is in the full tide of prosperity. He selects one hundred thousand pounds worth of the leading stocks, yielding at the price at which he purchased them, 6 per cent. At different banks where he keeps accounts for the purpose, he pawns the stock, and gets loans within 10 per cent.

<small>THE BEST OF ALL CHANCES FOR SPECULATOR WITH CAPITAL.</small>

of the market value, which amount to eighty thousand pounds. The ten thousand pounds he has himself, which enables him to take the stock off the market. In this way he is virtually the possessor for the time of this amount of stock, and he profits by the rise in value at the rate of one thousand pounds for every one per cent. Apart from this advantage he benefits to the extent of the difference between the yield on the money value of the stocks, and the interest with which the bankers debit him on the eighty thousand pounds; and so long as circumstances are favourable and the value of money does not rise and remain above the rate which the stocks yield, he enjoys an income from that source with a fair prospect in a year or so of doubling his ten thousand pounds

<small>THE MOST LEGITIMATE FORM OF SPECULATION, PAWNING THE STOCK.</small>

Very large amounts of money are known to have been made in 1870, 1871, and 1872, in English railway, and also in various other stocks, in this way in the London market, when money was poured in from France and the Continent generally on the outbreak of the Franco-German war. Bankers, moreover, were aware that the large amounts placed with them for safe keeping might be called for at any time, and sound Stock Exchange securities, upon which loans could be made from fortnight to fortnight, were very much in favour. In consequence of such operations as that referred to, prices were found upon several occasions to be very much inflated, resulting in some mischief and not a few failures.

In speculation of this nature, there is a time to begin and a time to leave off. When stocks have attained a reasonably high level of value as a result of the recovery of a country's industry, the chances for the speculator to profit by a continuous rise are of course gone, and he seeks in other directions to turn his capital to account; but the example we have given illustrates perhaps the most legitimate of all forms of speculation in Stocks, provided always the operator knows his business, and allows a sufficient margin for contingencies.

<small>WHEN TO BEGIN AND WHEN TO LEAVE OFF.</small>

The marked difference between Stock Exchange business and other kinds is, that it is the custom to pay cash for all bargains when the settlement takes place. Special delays may be agreed to between persons who know each other well, but it is quite the exception, and certainly should remain so, for credit is already quite sufficiently extended throughout all branches of trade and commercial affairs.

The one thing that keeps a tight rein on Stock Exchange operators is the test of their position which lies in fortnightly cash settlements. The very nature of the business affords such facilities for incurring very large liabilities by extensive operations in various securities, that if settlements by bill accomodation were permitted, extending over two or three months as in trade, hopeless confusion would soon be the result, apart from the temptation which an insolvent broker or jobber would lie under further to involve himself so long as he could get the credit. The remarkably few failures that take place among stock-jobbers and brokers, when it is considered how much risk they run, and to what a limited extent they can make themselves aware, in time to avoid complications, of

<small>TEST OF A SPECULATOR'S PECUNIARY POSITION.</small>

---

* As said before, the settlement in New York is daily.   H. W. R.

their clients' actual means, reflects much credit upon them as a class. At the same time it must be admitted that the custom of frequent cash settlements, by testing the actual position of all concerned, is the best possible safe-guard against operators getting out of their depth; and although business generally would be very seriously curtailed if the custom prevailed in all branches of commerce when distance did not make it impossible, there can be no doubt that a vast deal of mischief and dishonesty would be nipped in the bud.

CHAPTER IX.

SPECULATION WITHOUT CAPITAL.

WE will now suppose a familiar case of a speculator following in the path of so many wise persons who have gone before to their ruin in the process of applying some nostrum, which was to make their fortune in a week. The fortnightly settlements on the Stock Exchange take place about the middle and end of each month. We will suppose a young speculator, full of ideas upon such subjects, and having just sufficient knowledge of the different stocks to make believe that he knows a great deal, gets introduced to a broker, who on ascertaining that he has two or three hundred pounds available, intimates his willingness to execute his orders. The speculator buys £5,000 Turkish 5 per cents of 1865, £5,000 Spanish 3 per cents and £5,000 Egyptian 7 per cents of 1868, being told that these are easy markets to deal in. We will assume these bargains are done in the middle of an account. On the day of the purchases the several stocks rise ¼ to ½ per cent., and he goes home a happy man with his contracts in his pocket, reckoning the gain he has already made, and sleeps like a top. He rises with a light heart next morn-

A FAMILIAR CASE.

ing to devour his money article and breakfast simultaneously, eagerly searching in the list for his friends the Turkish, Spanish and Egyptian Stocks. The rise reported to him by his broker the evening before is confirmed in his newspaper, and he is in the act of laying it down when his eye catches a telegram, headed "Defeat and resignation of the French Government." His little experience has already taught him that the leading foreign stocks are largely dealt in on the Continent, and here comes a sinking of the heart number one. The breakfast is left unfinished, and he hurries to the city to find the Stock Markets open very flat all around on selling orders from Paris. The ¼ to ½ per cent. profit had disappeared, and an additional 1 per cent. into the bargain; so that instead of standing to gain £30 or £40, he stands to lose £150. A conference with the broker is somewhat encouraging, as he laughs over the matter, and assures his client that "they are bound to rally." Another day passes and there is no rally. Several days go by, and disorders in the streets are reported from Paris, causing further sales in the London market, and our friend sees a loss of £300 on his three purchases.* The "carrying over" day arrives without any recovery having taken place, but the broker is still cheerful, being himself a man of some means, although suffering from the prevalent disease of a great weakness for commissions, which has often caused him heavy losses through negligence in ascertaining the means of his clients. "It is only a question of seeing it out, sir," he says,

<small>BITTER EXPERIENCE.</small>

<small>THE QUESTION OF SEEING IT OUT.</small>

---

* All these experiences happen also in the New York Stock market, only in different form, such as railroad wars, law-suits, injunctions, &c.. H. W. R.

an observation which disperses with a lightning flash the ignorance under which our friend had hitherto labored with regard to the necessity of available capital, or in still plainer terms, ready cash. He goes away to turn this awkward dilemma in which he finds himself, over in his mind. Seeing it out, is, of course, waiting for a recovery. In the meantime he must pay his differences, which amount to £50 more than he possesses.

This one case in point tells the whole tale, and it is therefore superfluous to take up time and space with other instances. If legitimate trading business, in which the risk of loss is so reduced as to enable a man to earn a living at it, cannot be carried on without adequate capital, how is it possible that pure speculation can be successfully practised in which the conditions are reversed, and at which experience shows that no one can succeed except the professional expert, and only then in some cases under circumstances to which we have before referred?

CHAPTER X.

THE "TIP" TO BUY OR SELL.

A FOOL and his money are soon parted, is an old saw, and it is in a high degree applicable to the inexperienced speculator who operates in the markets on a friendly "tip."[*] It is marvellous to think how many persons daily and hourly are misled by the same snare and delusion. If a man, who starts off in an excited state to instruct his broker in consequence of having received the "tip" to buy a certain stock, pauses for one moment to reflect, he can hardly fail to doubt the disinterestedness of the communication. Take an example:—In the first place a man who gives a "tip" to another to buy some of a certain stock, must have some motive for so doing. No human being wanders about with, what he makes out to be, valuable information to distribute gratis among his friends. One might as well expect the girls who sell oranges, combs, umbrella-rings, and collar-studs, in Lombard Street, to give them away for nothing, as expect to obtain disinterested and genuine "tips" from some wandering philanthropist. Such a person was never heard of, and never will be. If a man gives the "tip" to

_{A FRIENDLY "TIP."}

---

* Point.   H. W. R.

buy a certain stock it is because he wants to "unload" at other people's expense,* and that is not what is generally understood by philanthropy. {UNLOADING AT OTHER PEOPLE'S EXPENSE.} The system of sending round the "tip" to buy or sell, has become very general in all markets. and it is certain that a vast deal of mischief is done by it. The common practice is for a number of persons to band together, and put the price of a certain article or stock up by buying a large quantity and making it scarce. When the higher price has been maintained for some little time, so that it meets the public eye in price currents, the process of putting the public in is commenced. When this benevolent operation has been sufficiently worked, and the "tip" has been administered to a number of poor dupes, the price is let down. Those who have advised their friend to buy, begin to sell and deliberately rob them, in return for the misplaced confidence.

There is a distinction between the qualified and the unqualified "tip." One man is a shade more honest than another, and does not exactly wish to charge his conscience with having {THE QUALIFIED "TIP."} deceived a friend with regard to a certain event. He merely suggests on general grounds that such a stock is going up. If he can get the person to whom the suggestion is made to act on such general advice, he achieves his purpose without exposing himself to be saddled with direct responsibility in case the result should be unfavourable. There are numbers of such persons who daily administer "tips," not only to their friends, but to strangers who will not trouble themselves to go farther to obtain any confirmation. Such

---

* Sometimes also for the purpose of encouraging first a following, and to unload later on. H W. R.

an important communication coming from credited quarters, is of course looked upon as a valuable secret to be acted on silently and immediately.

The unqualified "tip" comes from the individual who intends from the first to drive his horse full of armed men into the town, *vi et armis*, without too much parleying at the gates. He assumes an optimism of manner, and displays such a degree of confidence as shall override any rising objection, gets a promise to act on his advice, and passes on before the person to be made a tool of has time, or can summon courage, absolutely to refuse.

<small>THE UNQUALIFIED "TIP."</small>

Then there are "tips," worked by syndicates, which is a more elaborate affair. The extent of the increased area over which it is intended to operate depends upon the magnitude of the amount to be unloaded, the quality of the security, and the necessity for reaching a certain class of individuals. A vast deal of the rubbish that is shot away from the great financing centres is carefully and eagerly laid hold off by clergymen, and teachers male and female. As a rule, these good people seldom pause to reflect that what is so studiously brought under their notice in their rural retreats, is almost sure to lack a market anywhere else. Is it at all likely that so much trouble would be taken to recommend investments to people, by means of prospectuses delivered by the postman, if the statements contained in such prospectuses were really as true as they profess to be? In large cities there are innumerable agents for all country districts always on the look out for sound remunerative investments, and there is no need to recommend them to people's attention by thrusting them upon them at their own houses. Such a pro-

<small>"TIPS" WORKED TY SYNDICATES.</small>

cess of advertising is obviously to net the unwary, who are ignorant of what constitutes good security. The "tip" of a syndicate is passed on, so to speak, for a consideration, in proportion to the amount bought by the clients of the persons employed.

This branch of the subject can be almost indefinitely elaborated, but it may be concluded by one remark, which contains the pith of the whole thing, as applicable to speculation. Speculation as practised by the multitude is no better, in any market, than pitch and toss, and it is only by the aid of experience and more native skill, that some in the long run will lose less than others. One golden rule with reference to "tips," no matter from whom they proceed, or by what alleged incontrovertible facts they are supported, is this : when you are told to buy go and sell.

CHAPTER XI.

SPECULATION BY MACHINERY.

EVERYTHING, in these times, is done by machinery, and there is consequently no need for astonishment at finding that machinery is in existence for directing human volition. Such mechanism has for a long time been in working order, although it is scarcely realized by the community as a body. The most accomplished professional speculators make it their business to study the peculiar tendencies of people who have any money over and above what they immediately require for necessities. Firms, with numbers of clerks, exist in our day, who have forty, fifty, and as many sixty thousand names of people duly registered in their books, with their place of abode, duration of residences, means, style of living, trade, or profession, and other particulars, enabling a judgment to be formed of the kind of investment which is likely to suit them. These names are all duly marshalled under different heads, and when a certain kind of undertaking is to be brought before the notice of the public, in the form of a prospectus, that class of people for whom it is thought a suitable investment, have one sent to them by post. Experience has shown that it is unwise to scatter prospectuses

[marginalia: MACHINERY IN EXISTENCE FOR DIRECTING HUMAN VOLITION.]

broadcast over the country, trusting to some portion of them bringing applications. A wholesale scattering of prospectuses among a class of people who are not at all likely to read them even, will injure the credit of the scheme for which it is desired to raise the capital in proportion to the number of prospectuses that are thus wasted. As in everything else, in business great care must be taken to offer the right sort of investment to the persons addressed. A man, for instance who lives in a fine house in a country parish, owns land, and moves among the patricians of the district, would not think of looking at a new undertaking, if he knew a prospectus had come by the same post to a man who touches his hat to him, and lives in a small way outside the gates of the great man's estate. A man who is higher up in life than his neighbours endeavours, as a rule, to mark the distinction by having everything that belongs to him of a superior type. The man of high degree would consider himself insulted if he were classed indiscriminately with the man of low degree, in sending out twenty thousand prospectuses of a new mine. People are very touchy in such matters, and therefore, in catering for the public, as regards investments, great discrimination is necessary. The different classes of investors must be passed through the speculator's machine like the threshed corn, and when the husks and dust have been winnowed from the solid grain, he proceeds to classify them, and, as far as possible, learn their taste in the matter of investments.

<small>THE PATRICIAN INVESTOR.</small>

When joint-stock banking came into vogue, promoters of the new undertakings that were destined gradually to supersede private banks, and have superseded all but those that have exceptionally deep roots, and partners left who are very tenacious of ancient customs, were very tentative in their mode of proceeding. As with all new things for which the public require to be educated, companies established on the share system had in the beginning to be brought forward gently and quietly, so as not to startle people. Persons are easily scared when asked to become partners in a bank, in the sense of taking much responsibility and sharing but to a small extent in what are understood to be the honors of such a position. The finessing which was at first necessary to accustom the public to joint-stock undertakings was gradually followed by a thirst for shares, because all such concerns for a considerable time were associated with a premium. Individual promoters worked at the business of building up joint-stock schemes, then it grew to syndicates, and now we have wealthy firms, with large machinery, whose whole time and staff are devoted to hunting about the world for powers to bring out foreign loans, for concessions for making railways, docks, harbours, gasworks, and the like. When they have procured one or the other, they fix the amount of capital, cut it up into shares, and admin-

ADMINISTERING SHARES TO THE PUBLIC. ister them to the public, by much the same process as the Strasburgers enlarge the livers of their geese. Instead of people being asked politely by an advertisement to become shareholders in a new concern, the axiom of the supply creating a demand is acted upon in these times, and a man finds in his letter-box an investment especially suited to his taste and means, at the precise moment when his half-yearly dividends are falling due. The economy of capital is thus being pushed to its extremest limits, through the development of a system by which one man makes it his anxious business to see that his neighbour's interest on his capital shall scarcely have been passed to his credit at the bank before it is snatched away to fructify in some scheme for benefiting mankind in one or other of the four quarters of the globe..

Investments provided by machinery can be done on a very large scale, and when successful are as a consequence very profitable. But unfortunately it is a kind of avocation that is pretty nearly sure to be followed by many unscrupulous persons, who will resort to all kinds of deceit and trickery, in giving a false and dazzling hue to projects that should never have seen the light. Moreover, the great difficulty that individuals find in ascertaining the truth of statements, and the authenticity of facts, causes them too frequently to take for granted what should be always viewed with more or less suspicion, unless the people who vouch for such facts are of the most undoubted standing and respectability; and, as we have remarked, it is seldom that such persons will lend their names to anything of the kind. During a season of great prosperity the promotion of new companies is sure to be largely overdone, and great will be the losses suffered; but there is sure to be more good done in the world by the dissemination of capital in new parts of the earth that would otherwise lie for the most part unproductive, than there is harm done through the misapplication or loss of a part of it. Many people bewail and lament over the failure of a bank, a discount house, or joint-stock concern now and again, and when a commercial crisis takes place one would think the world was coming to an end, as indeed the Viennese thought when they had a sharp lesson for their money-greed, early in 1873; but a little sensible reflection will show that calms and storms alternate in every variety of form on the earth, and are not confined to seas whose strands occasionally strewed with the produce of a foreign clime is only an indication of the miscarriage of a minute portion of the benefits which, in fair weather, are conveyed by the inhabitants of one land to those of another.

The fact remains, however, that speculation by machinery, or in other words, the modern system of cramming the public with securities wholesale, may be attended with a good deal of mischief, and although it is too much to say that people who launch new undertakings upon such a system are necessarily unscrupulous, there are strong reasons for looking very closely at securities known to proceed from the offices of firms whose business it professedly is to make money by manufacturing stocks and shares wholesale, and forcing them upon the public. In the first place, such a business requires a great deal of money to carry it on, and a good deal of risk must be run, and money paid out of pocket, before there is a chance of seeing anything back again. Under such circumstances private enterprises are sought to be purchased at a small price, and sold to the public at a very large one, so as to secure a considerable margin, the only object of the speculators by machinery being to fill their own pockets.

It is astonishing what faith people put in printed certificates, got up in a style which resembles documents of real value. . A sheet of thin paper resembling that of a bank note, with a large impressed stamp of a corporation upon it, and filled in with the magic word sterling, is, as a rule, sufficient dust thrown in the eyes of the general public to send them home satisfied to make no further inquiries until collapse reveals the sham that has been prepared for them. Ordinary people go to market and make an elaborate fuss over a joint of meat before paying their money, seeing that it is to a Shylockian nicety of weight, but when they invest a hundred pounds in a mine, there have been cases in which they hardly knew where the property was,—or even if it existed at all. It is very wonderful that such an incomprehensible degree of confidence is placed in concoctors of companies, and it is the knowledge that the general public is so ludicrously gullible that encourages the formation of joint-stock concerns upon often the most flimsy bases.

CHAPTER XII.

THE SHIFTING OF SPECULATION FROM THE HIGHER TO THE LOWER CLASSES OF SECURITIES.

COMPARED with what there used to be in bygone years there is now next to no speculation in Consols at all. Merchants and bankers once upon a time used to speculate in the Funds* as a hedge. But things have changed, and such a method of *[SPECULATION IN CONSOLS AS A HEDGE.]* providing against a mercantile loss, which might be brought about by the same cause that would depress Consols, has gone out of fashion, doubtless owing in some degree to there being other modes of protecting themselves against risks which both merchants and bankers must for all time incur.

The maxim which is adopted by all prudent speculators in the markets, by which we mean the dealers in the Stock Exchange, who in the nature of their business must to some extent speculate, or they would lose business, is to sell when things are dear, and buy when they are cheap, and pay no attention at all to reports. Men who have had years of experience, know how to estimate at their just value the *on dits* that are for ever floating about their ears.

---

* Government Securities. H. W. R.

Right or wrong, there is no money in them in the long run, and it is with the long run that operators should have to do.

One reason why speculation in Consols has been reduced to a minimum is, that speculation has of late years changed its venue. The stock markets now are the field of operations for dealers in the stocks of all nations and all climes. There are a few countries whose names are still withheld from Wetenhall's list, among which China may be mentioned, but they are few. The extent to which the world has been borrowing within the last quarter of a century may be judged of from the fact that the indebtedness of the States of the world has increased from 1851 to 1873 by £2,218,000,000, the proportion of which belonging to Europe is £1,500,000,000. People have become used to making larger profits, by which we mean that all the world lives better and makes larger incomes than they used to. Consequently they do not care to speculate in stocks unless the fluctuations are somewhat considerable and frequent. The quieter attitude of England towards foreign states for many years past, and the absence of any internal disturbances worth mentioning, has produced much more steadiness in Government securities than was the case earlier in the century. There is not much exaggeration in the remark that a fluctuation of two per cent. in a day in Consols is now witnessed once in a life-time. The process of getting in and getting out of a stock, as a speculation, cannot be profitable when the fluctuations are so small and infrequent. Speculation consequently has

[sidenotes: Speculation has changed its venue. Increase of the indebtedness of the States of the world. The fluctuations in the price of Government stocks.]

shifted from the Consol market, and from the market where the highest class of securities is dealt in, to departments of the Stock Exchange where a bull or a bear stands to make something in a reasonable period, if he chance to be operating the right way. It may be supposed that speculation for this reason has decreased in extent. The contrary is the fact, speculators having simply taken up new ground, as they found it useless for any purpose to speculate in stocks in which the fluctuations were so small.

One of the reasons why speculation in high-class securities has more or less ceased is obviously because Consols and such like stocks are more firmly held than they used to be when the country was oftener engaged in wars, or disturbed by semi-revolutionary agitations. Then again, the very fact of high-class stocks remaining at a uniformly high level of price, causes a certain class of investors to buy them for simply absolute security's sake. There are numbers of people who hold Consols because they are perfectly certain their £3 odd per cent. per annum will always be paid.

<small>HIGH CLASS STOCKS MORE FIRMLY HELD THAN FORMERLY.</small>

They never trouble themselves about the price of the stock, and continue entirely apathetic whether the price rises to 120 or falls to 50. It stands to reason that, as the country grows in wealth, so do the holders of these high-class stocks increase in number, and as such securities are purchased largely for permanent holding, and purely as a means of providing income, so is steadiness imparted to the price, which tends consequently to be less and less disturbed in the absence of exceptionally adverse influences. There are always large numbers of persons in a country like England who are retiring from active life to live on an income, derived through the medium of public securities of one form or another, which is hereafter to be a purchasing power dependent upon the labour of others. One man does his share of work in the world, and in the process he provides for his future wants through the medium of saved capital. There can be no doubt that if the English national debt were to be paid off there would be a considerable commotion among those holders of Consols who would be satisfied with nothing else half as well. While the times in which we live therefore, continue quiet, the credit of the Government is firmly maintained, and the savings of the people are large, there will be always more buyers than sellers of high-class securities while the return for the money is not less than about 3 per cent. Buyers would in most cases probably prefer to look in other directions than pay anything over par for Consols. The fluctuations under such circumstances are consequently very small, and there is nothing literally but a bare bone for a speculator to pick, which is not worth the commission, and he migrates into other markets.

CHAPTER XIII.

THE SHORT "TURNS," OR, WHO MAKES THE PROFITS?

ALTHOUGH we have already alluded to this question of "turns," in referring to the forces, so to speak, in the markets which are arrayed against the speculator, we have thought it advisable, subsequently, to give it a separate chapter. The "turn" is a known quantity about which there is no doubt, and in which there is no element of chance to be reckoned upon according to any doctrine of probabilities, as sometimes favouring one side, and sometimes the other. The "turn" may be described in brief as the income of the jobber, or in other words that fractional part of the whole sum which, if a buyer of some stock, he gets by its sale in excess of what he pays—and if he be on the other hand, a seller, the "turn" is that proportional part of the whole sum which he gets in excess on buying back the stock, in order to square his book. Supposing the two operations of a purchase and a sale proceed first from a bull speculator, and secondly from a bear; the jobber in the one case covers himself as soon as he can by a purchase of the stock sold by the first operation, and by the sale of an amount equal to that bought by the second operation.

(marginal note: THE "TURN" A KNOWN QUANTITY ALWAYS AGAINST THE SPECULATOR.)

The "turn" comes in the second rank of obstacles which stand between the speculator and the goal, or profit, which it is his aim to reach, and is the most formidable of the fixed and, it may be said, inevitable, elements arrayed against him at the start. When a speculator enters the markets, therefore, he has to do his share of keeping both the broker and the jobber, and that not only when he commences his operations, but also when he finishes. There is the "turn" to be paid on going in, and also on coming out. The same may be said of the broker, only under certain circumstances. It is customary for a broker to charge no second commission on closing an operation, if it be done in the same account as that in which the operation was commenced. As speculators, however, especially the haphazard kind, are never contented to take small profits, and get out of the markets, they almost invariably pay a second commission. Thus there may be said to be two double fixed quantities, which are piled up against a speculator at the start.*

The Turn a Loss on Going Into and also in Coming Out of the Market.

If there be any difference in the character of the "turn" as compared with former times, it must be allowed that there is a point in favour of the speculator: whether it be more apparent than real, owing to the growth of other adverse influences is another matter. But it is certain that the "turn" is not so great in these times as it used to be, and it comes from the increase of competition by the larger number of jobbers in the markets, just as commissions in all

The Difference in the Character of the "Turn" as compared with Former Times.

---

* The usage at the New York Stock Exchange is different. H. W. R.

businesses have dwindled down from two and three per cent., and in some cases much more, to $\frac{1}{4}$ and $\frac{1}{8}$, and in the Stock markets to 1-16 and even a 1-32. It should, however, be remarked that, owing to the great increase in the number of transactions, the jobber makes more in these times by the smaller "turns" than he did formerly out of the large ones, the increase being in a greater ratio than the diminution in the amount of the single "turn." Moreover the public, as it is to be hoped should be the case with the growth of intelligence and the spread of education and wealth, decline to buy stocks when very wide prices are quoted to them from the jobbers. It stands to reason that the jobbers rather enjoy dealing in stocks where there is a good deal of cover for them to play with their prey. A difference of two or three per cent. between the buying and selling price affords the jobber much more scope in fixing the "turn" he is to get out of a transaction. The wide quotations between a buying and selling price are no doubt to some extent a legitimately justifiable defence against the sudden and perhaps violent fluctuations to which an indifferent security is exposed, and it is on this account the price is made wide. As the public, however, get to know and understand that a stock which is quoted say 35 to 38, as compared with one that is quoted 85 5-16 to 7-16 is in proportion to the difference between the extremes of the two figures, a worse security, so they instinctively avoid any operations at all where there is no knowing from one moment to the other whether their property is worth one per cent. more or less. In fact many young operators have been electrified to find that, having purchased on speculation some stock of the character of that quoted above at 35 to 38, and wishing to get out of the bargain, for some reason or other, there was a difference between the buying and the selling price of actually as much as that indicated, viz.: 3 per cent. Ruinous mistakes by the unwary are thus made. They fancy very naturally that a stock which is subject to violent fluctuations, and which is seen to fall and rise two or three per cent. in a day, is a fine field to operate in; but the compensation which is in all things, soon reveals itself here in the manner described, so that the speculator stands perhaps even less chance of making a profit off a widely fluctuating security than he would by one that moved to a smaller extent over or under a central point of value from which there was not so much movement. *Special Danger of Speculating in a Stock that is Quoted very wide.*

Then again, a jobber is willing to take a much smaller "turn" on a transaction which he can depend upon closing in his own book at any moment, at probably only a fractional difference in price from that at which he opened it. A speculator wishes, for instance, to buy £10,000 Consols for the rise at 92½. At the time the transaction is done the jobber knows he can any moment square his book as far as that operation is concerned, within a trifle of the same figure, and he is accordingly satisfied with a small "turn."

On the other hand, a stock that fluctuates violently may leave a buyer of it a loss of one or two per cent. before he has entered the operation in his book. The consequence is that a speculator proposing to buy for the rise £2,000 of a stock which is quoted in the markets at 35 to 38, will have probably to pay 38 or near about that for it, for the simple reason that the jobber who sells knows that a widely-quoted stock is liable to unusual movements in both directions, and he protects himself accordingly, by declining to sell except at the higher figure, or to buy except at or below the lowest. The difference may even be wider than in this hypothetical case. The stock may recently have become very much depreciated in value, which carries with it the obvious suggestion that it may fall still further indefinitely, short of the bottom, for reasons which have so far contributed to depress it. Under such circumstances, unless the jobbers in the markets have limits at which to buy such a security, they probably will refuse to purchase from an outside seller, or from anybody, at any price, unless it come within the range of a fancy figure. With stocks, therefore, that are liable to sudden and considerable changes in value, the "turn" assumes dimensions in proportion, and speculation in such securities is correspondingly dangerous.

For every operation that a speculator enters upon, he contributes to the income of the jobber. Although this statement is perhaps not literally accurate, inasmuch as the jobber may sometimes have to sacrifice his "turn," and even more, in selling stocks which he has bought in the course of his business, or in buying back stock which he has sold, it is sufficiently accurate as demonstrating the position of the speculator. Whether or not subsequent circumstances deprive the jobber of the turn he considers himself in the ordinary course of events to have secured, the speculator has in any case paid it, which is all we are concerned to show.*

THE "TURN" THE INCOME OF THE JOBBER.

---

* The real type of the London Jobber does not, however, exist in the New York Stock market.   H. W. R.

CHAPTER XIV.

IN THAT RESPECT IS SPECULATION USEFUL IN MARKETS GENERALLY?

THE remarks upon speculation in the foregoing chapters may, perhaps, lead the reader to infer that our object has been to enter upon a crusade against all speculators, *guerre à mort*. Such an impression would not be a correct one, and this chapter is intended, just in conclusion, to show why. Speculation in the sense of buying for cash or on ordinary credit what the purchaser has very good reason for knowing is uncommonly cheap, and what he believes will, ere long, improve in price, does not come under the category of speculation such as that to which the foregoing remarks refer. There is hardly an individual who buys anything who is not at times more or less of a speculator, and he has a perfect right so to be under given conditions, and his being so under such conditions is a direct benefit also to the community. For instance, take a very homely article which will serve for an illustration, bacon. Supposing bacon, through some passing influence, were to fall considerably in price, very large purchases would at once be made on speculation, because it is an article

<small>SPECULATION FOR THE RISE, WHICH IS BOTH LEGITIMATE AND OF BENEFIT TO THE COMMUNITY.</small>

almost certain to be directly consumed in a proportion greater than the production could be increased. Large quantities would be taken off the market by both retail and wholesale dealers, who would store it in anticipation of a recovery in value. They probably would not want it for immediate use, and would be induced to run the risk of the operation turning out profitable by reason of its being suddenly so much cheaper than they had been accustomed to buy it. They would, in one word, speculate in bacon, just as some people speculate in stocks after a heavy fall. Unless something had happened to permanently depreciate the value of bacon this rush of buyers, the great majority of whom would soon settle their operations by cash payments, would speedily cause at least a partial recovery in value, which might be followed by a further rise or relapse according to circumstances. Whether anything serious had been at work to depreciate value or not, the innumerable interests that would have suffered by the decline in value would thus be protected at least for a time by the speculative operations referred to. The price would be kept up above what it would have been in the absence of such speculative operations, while either the real or fictitious agency at work in causing a fall were discovered and analysed. So in

Speculation for the fall, which is both legitimate and of benefit to the community.

a converse sense, if for some reason or other the price of corn were driven up very rapidly several shillings per quarter above the value ruling at a particular period, without holders of large stocks being able to discover sufficient cause, many of them would hurry to market and sell what was still even unthrashed. They would be so tempted by the very high price that they would speculate upon such a high quotation being followed by a low one, and they would sell all they could manage to deliver in a given time. The speculator in the bacon would be playing in a legitimate sense the part of the bull, and the speculator in corn that of the bear. It will be admitted that there is what we know as a reasonable price for all things, and that it is better for all concerned that a reasonable relative value is maintained for all articles than that anything becomes either extravagantly dear or so cheap that it is worth no one's while to produce it. Every article of those consumed by mankind in their several stations has its fitting place either as a necessity or as a luxury. A necessity for some reason may in course of time become a luxury, while, what is much oftener the case, luxuries may by degrees come under the category of necessities. The value of the one or the other may in relation to other necessities or luxuries change, but it will probably change only gradually, and during the process of change there will be a reasonable relative value for such articles. It is important then in order to satisfy the rational desires of all members of the community that the reasonable relative values of all commodities should, if disturbed by any cause, remain so as short a time as possible. The undue inflation or depression of prices will be counteracted by speculative operations such as we have referred to, and in that sense, speculation is directly of immense benefit, as it is one limb of a body of law which administers justice silently but surely to any one who has left one weak point in his armour when attempting by violent or fraudulent means to snatch a profit by unjustifiably raising or depressing prices. The one condition,

A REASONABLE RELATIVE VALUE FOR ALL COMMODITIES.

however, of such speculation being of direct benefit in keeping prices at a level which is in accord with the existing state of supply in relation to the demand at any period is, that the speculative operations shall partake as nearly as possible of the nature of *bona fide* operations. The great benefit which is caused by the one kind of speculation is the antithesis of the evil which results from the system of " time-bargain " speculation as practised in all markets. The one kind of speculation is the legitimate advantage taken of being able to buy any article cheap, or to sell any commodity that is dear, whereas the other is nothing better than pitch and toss in disguise.

The kind of speculation which is of benefit to the community may be termed corrective speculation, as implying a restoration of prices, through its agency, to a reasonable relative level: Such speculation would come from buyers who had good reason to know that what they bought they would be able again to sell, and that its purchase speculatively was simply the supply of their ordinary requirements in anticipation, owing to a favourable opportunity having presented itself. In proportion as speculation proceeds from simply time-bargain operators will the price be driven up or down, according to circumstances, to an injurious degree, as compared with a corrective degree, the influence of the one set of speculators doing good, and that of the other set harm.

Speculators may be divided into three classes which about embraces all the phases of speculation. First, we have the legitimate speculator who spends all or some of his surplus capital in taking off the market what he

<small>THE THREE CLASSES INTO WHICH SPECULATORS MAY BE DIVIDED</small>

believes will give him a gain by holding it for some time. That is the legitimate speculator who is a benefit to the community as a leveller up of prices. Then we have the legitimate speculator of the same stamp, with a difference that he is a leveller down of prices, and is equally of service to society by immediately throwing on the market all the stock of a certain article he may hold or be able to get for the purpose, when it rises to a price above what he calculated on being able to obtain, and which his experience told him was an unusually high figure. Such speculators as these not only do not hurt themselves, but directly benefit themselves by speculating, and in so doing protect the interests of their neighbours and the community at large. Such as these this book is not written for. We are concerned with those who, classified as illegitimate speculators, and reckless speculators, which, second term may have to be moved a point or two according to circumstances, are over the border-line, whose *dictum* is "Heads I win, tails you lose." The illegitimate speculator is the one who starts with a small capital and with some method, with the idea of increasing it upon a system of incurring risks which, in the ordinary course of the market he may operate in, will enable him in case he has wrongly calculated the course of prices, to pay his losses and go on again. His intention is never *bona fide* sale or *bona fide* purchase. The reckless speculator is the man who with little more than he stands up in makes a great pretence, imposes upon the weak and credulous, enters the Stock markets and operates to right and left up to the hilt so far as he may be trusted. So long as he may enjoy a run of luck he rakes in the coin;

when it turns he leaves his dupes to pay and goes up the country, as they say of the native Indian merchants when the telegraph announces to them that the goods shipped to Europe for which they have drawn, will leave a loss.

We have then one class of speculators which is of direct use and value in all markets, while the other two, the nature of whose operations we have endeavoured to lay bare, cause an infinite deal of mischief, and get in ninety-nine cases out of a hundred no good for themselves in the long run, whether their transactions are entered upon carelessly, and are allowed simply to take their chance, or an attempt be made to achieve success by some exercise or skill.

OPINION AS TO VALIDITY OF "PUTS," "CALLS," &c.

Law Offices of SIMON STERNE.
29 Willliam Street,
NEW YORK, July 24th, 1886.

H. W. ROSENBAUM, ESQ.,
60 Exchange Place, New York,

DEAR SIR :

You ask my opinion as to time contracts known as "puts, "calls," and "straddles" or "spreads," in relation to stocks, bonds, etc. The inquiry is prompted by the apprehension that such contracts may be regarded by the law as of a gambling character, and therefore not enforceable.

Contracts partake of the nature of wagers only when there is no intention either to deliver or to receive the goods, stocks, or bonds, which form the subject matter of the contract. That in point of fact and as a matter of local custom, differences are sometimes paid on the settlement of time contracts instead of delivery being actually made, does not affect the original transaction, and does not invalidate it. So long as there was not a clear intention, either express or implied, that the things themselves were not, under any circumstances, either to be called for or to be delivered, and so long as the holder of the "call" has the right to demand the actual delivery of the stocks or bonds mentioned in the contract, or the holder of the "put" has the right to insist upon the actual delivery of the stocks, bonds or merchandise represented by the "put," the transaction can, in no sense, be considered a gambling one or partake of the nature of a wager, although, instead of the actual delivery, differences may and sometimes are, as a matter of compromise, accepted for convenience, at the time when the contract is to be enforced.

This practice of paying differences is, as I understand it, much rarer, however, than the actual delivery of the stocks or bonds mentioned in the contract. The courts have of late years, with great uniformity, dealt with these contracts with the disposition to uphold and maintain them, and have discredited the defence of their being of the nature of a wager, and have held the contracting parties to their agreements in the same manner as in every other contract for which a reasonable consideration had passed.

The decision of the Courts of this State, of Massachusetts, Pennsylvania and Illinois, and in the Federal tribunals, where, in one form or another, these contracts have been the subject matter of examination, have been so uniform in that direction that we can now regard this as settled law.

It was only in the infancy of those larger and more complicated mercantile transactions incident upon the development of the modern industrial world, that doubts as to the moral aspect of these contracts could arise. Political science proves, and the law has followed the conclusion, that these time contracts now form a necessary part and perform a conservative function in the economy of a fully developed commercial life. They are an as yet undeveloped form of insurance of values to a purchaser, for which the purchaser pays a fair equivalent, and in process of time such insurances must perform a larger and more important function in the purchase of commodities or of representatives of value which have a tendency to fluctuate largely in price.

For a time it was supposed that the ordinary policy of fire insurance partook of the nature of a bet, and there was doubt as to whether the Courts would enforce contracts of insurance, because it looked as though the insurer was saying to a man who wanted to have his house insured against fire, "I will bet you the value of you house that it does not burn down." But we have long since departed from this infantile mode of looking at the situation and have learned to regard insurance as one of the conservative elements of modern civilized life, by which heavy losses are evenly distributed instead of coming with crushing effect upon the persons suffering the misfortune.

The capitalist who sells a "put" or a "call" performs precisely the same function as an insurer. He receives an equivalent therefor, and it is a means by which he can turn the securities in his hands with an intermediate profit, without serious risk, except that in the case of a "call" he may be compelled to change the character of his securities, or replace the securities which he has called from him, and in the case of a "put" he may be compelled to re-acquire the securities that he has parted with; but, distributed over a very large mass, and through different classes, of securities, these "calls" and "puts" will balance themselves and leave, if intelligently pursued, a resultant profit to the operator in the "puts" and "calls," with a prevention of disaster to the purchaser of the privileges, as against excessive fluctuations in the market.

Respectfully yours,

SIMON STERNE.

H. W. ROSENBAUM,

60 EXCHANGE PLACE, NEW YORK,

Broker and Dealer in Options on Bonds and Stocks

Besides the usual Options (Puts, Calls and Spreads) with prices fixed at a certain distance from the market price of the Stocks or Bonds, I devote especial attention to the negotiation of Options (Puts, Calls and Straddles), with price fixed at the current market price of the Stocks, etc., which latter class of Options my experience has proven to be the most advantageous and ultimately cheapest.

I will also contract *Insurances against loss* on purchases or short sales of Stocks or Bonds, made through me, during periods ranging from one week to sixty days, and in quantities of from 100 shares ($10,000 Bonds), upwards.

The Premiums to be paid for such Insurance range from $112.50 per 100 shares upwards, according to length of time and character of security, and cover the whole loss which the speculator may incur on this transaction.

Circulars, Rates and Information furnished on application.

H. W. ROSENBAUM,

60 Exchange Place, New York.

www.ingramcontent.com/pod-product-compliance
Lightning Source LLC
Chambersburg PA
CBHW022125160426
43197CB00009B/1159